The U. S. Colored Troops
at
Andersonville Prison

By
Bob O'Connor

INFINITY
PUBLISHING.COM

Copyright © 2009 by Bob O'Connor

Unlike my other three books,
this is a work of non-fiction.

ISBN 0-7414-5767-9

Published by:

PUBLISHING.COM

1094 New DeHaven Street, Suite 100
West Conshohocken, PA 19428-2713
Info@buybooksontheweb.com
www.buybooksontheweb.com
Toll-free (877) BUY BOOK
Local Phone (610) 941-9999
Fax (610) 941-9959

Printed in the United States of America

Published January 2010

Dedication

To my father, Charles L. O'Connor aka
"Cheerful Charlie" who died in 1993.
Thanks, Dad, for teaching me the importance
of integrity, hard work and always seeing
the job through until the end.

Foreword

To a Civil War prisoner early in the war, prison was a place to stay for several days before you were exchanged. It was no big deal.

It the latter stages of the war, Union General Ulysses S. Grant cancelled the exchange. The Union Army had an over-abundance of troops and supplies compared to General Lee, who had few soldiers and even less supplies. General Grant sacrificed his Union troops in Confederate prisons to block returning rebel troops to the front to aid his opponent.

Confederate and Union prisons became "hell holes" as the men suffered the consequences of being in places holding far too many prisoners for what the stockades were originally built to accommodate.

Andersonville, though not the only prison where soldiers wasted away and became living skeletons, was certainly one of the most famous Civil War prisons.

Though it was rare that a black soldier ended up in any Confederate prison, Andersonville held more than ten percent of all U.S. Colored prisoners in the conflict.

All soldiers on both sides are heroes. The U.S. Colored troops at Andersonville Prison are among them. For some reason, their story has slipped through the cracks and has not been told.

This book is a long overdue tribute to those brave black soldiers who endeavored to overcome the hardships of prison life at Andersonville. About a third of the USCT soldiers there didn't make it out alive. Thankfully all but one of the USCT soldiers who died there has a marked grave at the prison cemetery with his name and regiment, in what is today a National Park in Andersonville, Georgia.

Those who did make it out were scarred for life, both physically and psychologically, and were often not recognized by their loved ones.

It is a sad, but true legacy, of man's inhumanity to man.

Table of Contents

U.S. Colored Troops

Even though colored men had fought in both the Revolutionary War and the War of 1812, a federal law in 1791 prohibited blacks from serving in either state militias or the U.S. Army.[1] In fact, the first casualty of the Battle of Bunker Hill in Revolutionary War was Crispus Attucks, a black man.[2]

As early as May 1861, Frederick Douglass, noted black leader, implored President Lincoln to "carry the war to Africa" by saying "let the slaves and free colored people be called into service, and formed into a liberating army."[3] But Lincoln held off, fearing the border states would leave the Union if blacks were taken into the army. President Lincoln said "the nation could not afford to lose at this crisis" and by arming blacks, "would turn 50,000 bayonets from the loyal Border states against us that were for us."[4]

Union General Benjamin Butler, that same month, refused to return three fugitive slaves to their southern plantation owners, declaring them "contrabands of war." He asserted that they could be seized by the government. Congress saw to that logic in the First Confiscation Act of August 6, 1861, declaring that the army could confiscate property, including slaves, who were employed by the states in rebellion.[5]

---

[1] Black Soldiers in Blue, pg. 9 and www.redstone.army.mil/history/integrate/CHRON1.html – Congress passed a law prohibiting both blacks and Native Americans from peacetime militia. In May 1792 additional legislation called for only white male citizens to serve in the militia. All state militia laws reflected the same policy. Among reasons given were fears of slave rebellions, African Americans would not or could not fight, the idea that service by blacks would cause undesirable social change, and that if blacks were armed it would be a sign that white soldiers had failed.

[2] www.pbs.org/wgbh/aia/part2/2p24.html

[3] Black Soldiers in Blue, pg. 9

[4] Strike the Blow for Freedom, pg. 1

[5] African American Soldier in the Civil War, USCT 1862-66, pg. 4

By authorization of the Second Confiscation Act of July 17, 1862 (Section 12) and the Militia Act of the same date (Sections 12, 13, and 15) Congress "authorized the President to receive into service of the United States, for the purpose of construction of entrenchments or performing camp duty, or any labor, or any military or naval service for which they were found to be competent, persons of African descent, and provided that such persons should be enrolled and organized, under such regulations nor inconsistent with the Constitution and laws as the President might prescribe."[6]

The intent was to allow the use of blacks as teamsters and laborers. But the actual result went beyond that, as Union generals attempted to enlist black soldiers to fill their depleting ranks.[7]

The first official authorization to use colored troops occurred following the passage of the Second Confiscation Act and the Militia Order. Even with those official designations, the use of the colored troops received a plethora of treatments and reactions. In the Departments of Tennessee and in the South, the USCT were frequently used for fatigue work. In the eastern theater, the USCT were used both in combat and for fatigue work, even though the president did not officially approve the use of the colored regiments for combat until he issued the Emancipation Proclamation on January 1, 1863.[8]

The first black regiments were formed in late 1862 and early 1863 and included the 1st South Carolina Volunteer Infantry, the 1st, 2nd and 3rd Louisiana Native Guard, the 1st Louisiana Heavy Artillery and the 1st Regiment of the Kansas Infantry.[9] In August of 1862, Kansas Senator Jim Lane enlisted colored soldiers in the 1st Kansas Colored Infantry. The 1st Kansas Volunteer mustered into service in

---

[6] Men of Color, pg. 1
[7] African American Soldier in the Civil War, USCT 1862-66, pg. 5
[8] Publication Number M-1821, pg. 1
[9] Men of Color, pg. 1 and Publication Number M-1821, pg. 1

January 1863 became the first black regiment from a northern state.[10]

On September 2, 1862, the Cincinnati Black Brigade was organized as an unarmed labor force. General Butler organized the Louisiana Native Guard on September 27, 1862.[11]

In his preliminary Emancipation Proclamation issued following the Union victory at Sharpsburg, Maryland in September, 1862, the President told Congress, "And as a fit and necessary military measure, for effecting this purpose, I, as Commander-in-Chief of the Army and Navy of the United States, do order and declare, on the first day of January in the year of our Lord one thousand eight hundred and sixty-three, all persons held as slaves within any state or states, wherein the constitutional authority of the United States shall not then be practically recognized, submitted to and maintained, shall then, thenceforward, and forever, be free."[12]

The 1st Kansas Colored Infantry first saw action at Island Mount, Missouri on October 27, 1862.[13]

In October, 1862, General Rufus Saxton became the first person to raise a regiment of former slaves to fight in the Union Army with the sanctions of the War Department and Secretary Stanton.[14] Even though the 1st South Carolina Infantry (men of African descent) was not organized officially until January of 1863, three of the regiment's companies saw action on coastal expeditions as early as November, 1862.[15]

On January 1, 1863, with President Lincoln's Emancipation Proclamation, called General Order No. 1, one paragraph specifically addressed the colored troops, saying "such persons of suitable condition will be received into the armed service of the United States, to garrison forts,

---

[10] Black Soldiers in Blue, pg. 20
[11] African American Soldier in the Civil War, USCT 1862-66, pgs. 7 & 8
[12] Strike a Blow for Freedom, pg. 3
[13] Publication Number M-1821, pg. 1
[14] Black Soldiers in Blue, pg. 22
[15] Publication Number M-1821, pg. 1

positions, stations and other places, and to man vessels of all sorts in said service."[16]

By the beginning of 1863, Secretary of War Edwin Stanton authorized the raising of U.S. Colored regiments in Connecticut, Rhode Island and Massachusetts – but denied the same in Ohio. John Mercer Langston, William Birney, Martin R. Delany, Richard P. Hallowell, Henry McNeal Turner, George L. Stearns, and Frederick Douglass, all abolitionists, were commissioned by the war department to recruit black troops.[17]

On January 26, 1863, Massachusetts Governor John A. Andrew petitioned the War Department for permission to raise colored troops. Secretary of War Stanton approved the request. The 54th and 55th Massachusetts regiments were thereby organized. Lacking a sufficient number of the black volunteers in Massachusetts, recruiters targeted Philadelphia blacks to fill the rolls. Philadelphia was a city that had the largest black population of any city in the free states.[18] By late June, the *Philadelphia Inquirer* estimated that 1500 black men from Philadelphia had already enlisted in the two Massachusetts colored regiments.[19] A Philadelphia man, Norwood Pemrose Hallowell, was assigned as commander of the 55th Massachusetts.[20]

Around the same time, Mr. Stanton ordered General Lorenzo Thomas to go into the lower Mississippi River Valley to enlist free and contraband colored troops. Stanton wanted all white officers for the colored regiments, but did allow blacks to enlist as chaplains and surgeons.[21]

On May 1, 1863, the Confederate Congress authorized Jefferson Davis to have captured officers of colored regiments be "put to death or to be otherwise punished at the discretion of military tribunals." At the same

---

[16] Lincoln's Emancipation, Black Soldiers in Blue, pg. 1
[17] Black Soldiers in Blue, pgs. 24 & 25
[18] Strike a Blow for Freedom, pg. 5
[19] Ibid
[20] Ibid, pg. 6
[21] Publication Number M-1821, pgs. 1 & 2

time, they declared that colored enlisted men were to "be delivered to the authorities of the State or States in which they shall be captured to be dealt with accordingly to the present or future laws of such State or States." This meant the colored soldiers could be sold into slavery or put to death.[22]

[22] The Negro's Civil War, pg. 174

The Bureau of Colored Troops

In May, 1863, the War Department issued Order Number 143 which set up the Bureau of Colored Troops. The department assigned Assistant Adjutant General Charles W. Foster to oversee the recruitment of colored troops and to secure officers to command them.[23] The Bureau's responsibilities included recruiting colored troops, appointing officers to command those regiments, and maintaining all the records for those regiments.[24] All units mustered in were placed under USCT federal designation except for regiments from Massachusetts, Connecticut and Louisiana.[25]

General Order No. 143
War Department
Adjutant General's Office
Washington May 22, 1863

I.   A Bureau is established in the Adjutant General's Office for the record of all matters relating to the organization of Colored Troops. An officer will be assigned to the charge of the Bureau, with such number of clerks as may be designated by the Adjutant General.

II.   Three or more field officers will be detailed as Inspectors to supervise the organization of colored troops at such points as may be indicated by the War Department in the Northern and Western States.

III.   Boards will be convened at such posts as may be decided upon by the War

---

[23] Black Soldiers in Blue, pgs. 26 & 28

[24] Man of Color, pg. 3

[25] Black Soldiers in Blue, pg. 28

Department to examine applicants for commissions to command colored troops, who, on application to the Adjutant General, may receive authority to present themselves to the board for examination.

IV. No person shall be allowed to recruit colored troops except specifically authorized by the War Department; and no such authority will be given to persons who have not been examined and passed by a board, nor will such authority be given any one person to raise more than one regiment.

V. The reports of Boards will specify the grade of commission for which each candidate is fit, and authority to recruit will be given in accordance. Commissions will be issued from the Adjutant General's Office when the prescribed number of men is ready for muster into service.

VI. Colored troops may be accepted by companies, to be afterwards consolidated in battalions and regiments by the Adjutant General. The regiments will be numbered *seriatim*, in the order in which they are raised, the numbers to be determined by the Adjutant General. They will be designated " _____ Regiment of U.S. Colored Troops."

VII. Recruiting stations and depots will be established by the Adjutant General as circumstances shall require, and officers will be detailed to muster and inspect the troops.

VIII. The non-commissioned officers of colored troops may be selected and appointed from the best men of their number in the usual mode of appointing non-commissioned officers. Meritorious commissioned officers will be entitled to promotion to higher rank if they prove themselves equal to it.

IX. All personal applications for appointments in colored regiments, or for information concerning them, must be made to the Chief of the Bureau; all written communications should be addressed to the Chief of the Bureau, to the care of the Adjutant General.

By the order of the Secretary of War
E.D. Townsend, Assist. Adj. General[26]

The Bureau of Colored Troops was established to be responsible for "all matters relating to the organization of Colored Troops." At this time, all new units were to be designated as United States Colored Troops. Those already established with state designations such as the 54th Massachusetts Infantry, the 55th Massachusetts Infantry, the 19th Connecticut Infantry, the 6th Louisiana Infantry, the 7th Louisiana Infantry, the 3rd Tennessee Volunteer Infantry, the 5th Massachusetts Cavalry, and the 1st South Carolina Volunteers were allowed to keep their state names.[27]

The first regiments were named as federal efforts because states were not willing to claim the black troops. Thus they were numbered as the 1st U.S. Colored Infantry Regiment, and the like.[28]

The first official war action the USCT were involved in took place on May 27, 1863 when the 1st and 3rd Louisiana Native Guard regiments (also known as the *Corps d'Afrique*) fought at Port Hudson, Louisiana. The fighting involved free negroes and former slaves from Louisiana. These USCT

---

[26] United States Colored Troops, 1863-1867, pg. 17
[27] Publication Number M-1821, pg. 2
[28] African American Soldier in the Civil War, USCT 1862-66, pgs. 6 & 7

recruits were amongst the troops who assaulted Port Hudson, a Confederate position of strength along the lower Mississippi.

Representative Charles A. Wickliffe, Kentucky, voiced the sentiments of many from both the North and the South saying blacks were unfit for military enlistment of any kind and that "a negro is afraid, by instinct or by nature, of a gun."[29] Others questioned the black's courage, and ability to be a soldier.

The following is part of the record of the battle that ensued: "The self-forgetfulness, the undaunted heroism, and the great endurance of the negro, as exhibited that day, created a new chapter in American history for the colored man."[30]

A white officer who witnessed the battle later said: "You have no idea how my prejudices in regard to negro troops have been dispelled by the battle the other day. The brigade of negroes behaved magnificently and fought splendidly; could not have done better. They are far superior in discipline to the white troops and just as brave."[31]

And the *New York Times* reporter at the same battle told his readers, "this official testimony settles the question that the negro race cannot fight... It is no longer possible to doubt the bravery and steadiness of the colored race, when rightly led."[32]

By this time Frederick Douglass was in full support, urging blacks to enlist. He said, "Never since the world began was a better chance offered to a long enslaved and oppressed people. The opportunity is given us to be men. With one courageous resolution we may blot out the hand-writing of the ages against us. Once let the black man get on his person the brass letters U.S.; let him get an eagle on his button, and a musket on his shoulder, and bullets in his

---

[29] Black Soldiers in Blue, pg. 10
[30] The Negro's Civil War, pg. 185
[31] Ibid
[32] Ibid

pocket, and there is no power on the earth or under the earth which can deny that he has earned the right of citizenship in the United States. I say again, this is our chance, and woe betide us if we fail to embrace it."[33]

By the Spring of 1863, Confederate Secretary of War James Seddon issued the policy that his department "determined that negroes captured will not be regarded as prisoners of war" and later declared that any white officer recruiting, commanding or training colored troops would be "deemed as inciting servile insurrection, and shall, if captured, be put to death or to be otherwise punished at the discretion of the court." [34]

The Lincoln Administration responded with Order No. 100 stating that the black soldiers and their officers should be respected as soldiers and treated as prisoners of war. The order said if the black soldier was a slave who entered the North as a fugitive, they were "immediately entitled to the rights and privileges of a freeman." The order stated that all soldiers without regard to color or class were organized into military units, and they must be treated as "public enemies" and not individuals. The order also insisted that since international law had no color distinctions, enslavement or sale of captured blacks would demand retaliation of death from this crime against the nations.[35]

The *Anglo-American* newspaper, on July 11, 1863, issued the following:

"White Americans Remember! that we know that in going to the field we neither get bounty, or as much wages even as you receive for performance of the same duties; that we are well aware of the facts that if captured we will be treated like wild beasts by our enemies; that the avenue to honor and promotion is closed to us; but for these things we care not. We fight for

---

[33] Black Soldiers in Blue, pg. 28
[34] Ibid, pg. 45
[35] Ibid, pg. 46

God, liberty and country, not money. We will fight fearless of capture, as we do not expect quarter so we shall give none. It is infinitely more honorable to die upon the battle field, than to be murdered by the barbarians of the South. Promotion we will not ask, until we have earned it; and when we have, this nation shall know no rest until those in authority have crowned their brow of our heroes with wreaths of living green; until the highway of advancement is open to the dusky sons of America, as well as those of paler hue.[36]

On July 18, 1863, the 54th Massachusetts USCT once again proved the colored troops were courageous, determined, and willing to die for their country. A *New York Tribune* reporter said the stand the 54th Massachusetts made by not faltering, "made Fort Wagner such a name to the colored race as Bunker Hill has been for ninety years to the white Yankees."[37]

On July 31, 1863, President Lincoln issued Order No. 252 which declared that the government would protect all its soldiers who became prisoners of war, regardless of color.

The president further explained that "to sell or enslave any captured person on account of his color and for no offense against the laws of war, is a relapse into barbarism and a crime against the civilization of the age." He ordered that "for every soldier of the United States killed in violation of the laws of war, a rebel soldiers shall be executed, and for everyone enslaved by the enemy or sold into slavery, a rebel soldier shall be placed at hard labor…until the other shall be released and received the treatment due to a prisoner of war."[38]

Because of their desperation for filling enlistment quotas with soldiers, colored men were often promised both

[36] The Negro's Civil War, pg. 182
[37] Ibid, pg. 191
[38] Black Soldiers in Blue, pg. 47

pay and their freedom.[39] Colored men were also eligible to serve as substitutes for whites who had been drafted.[40] Those black men who were physically unable to serve were often enlisted in invalid corps and placed on garrison duty.[41]

By August, 1863, there were fourteen colored regiments ready for service or already in the field with an additional twenty-four in the process of being formalized. Of the fourteen regiments who were ready, five had been mustered in from the North.[42] And by the end of that same month, General August Banks had already enlisted almost 15,000 black soldiers in Louisiana.[43]

In a private letter to President Lincoln on August 23, 1863, General Ulysses S. Grant said, "I have given the subject of arming the negro my hearty support. This, with the emancipation of the negro, is the heavyest (sic) blow yet given the Confederacy...By arming the negro we have added a powerful ally. They will make good soldiers and by taking them from the enemy weakens him in the same proportion they strengthen us. I am therefore most decidedly in favor of pushing this policy to the enlistment of a force sufficient to hold all the South falling into our hands and to aid in capturing more."[44]

To aid recruiting of colored troops in the states of Missouri, Tennessee, Kentucky and Maryland, Genera Order No. 329 was issued by the War Department on October 3, 1863 which stated that persons willing to offer his or her slave into military service, would "if such slave be accepted, receive from the recruiting officer a certificate thereof, and become entitled to compensation for the service of labor of said slave, not exceeding three hundred dollars, upon filing a

---

[39] African American Soldier in the Civil War, USCT 1862-66, pg. 10
[40] Ibid, pg. 13
[41] Ibid
[42] The Negro's Civil War, pg. 172
[43] Ibid, pg. 170
[44] Ibid, pg. 191

valid deed of manumission and of release, and making satisfactory proof of title."[45]

By October, 1863, there were 37,482 colored troops (including their white officers) in 58 colored regiments. The men were from the District of Columbia, seven Confederate states and eight Northern states including Maryland.[46]

Frederick Douglass continued to give his support of colored enlistments in his writings. He stated emphatically, "Shall colored men enlist notwithstanding this unjust and ungenerous barriers raise against them? We answer yes. Go into the army and go with a will and a determination to blot out this and all other mean discriminations against us. To say we won't be soldiers because we can't be colonels is like saying we won't go into the water till we have learned to swim. A half a loaf is better than no bread – and to go into the army is the speediest and best way to overcome the prejudices which has dictated unjust laws against us. To allow us in the army at all, is a great concession. Let us take this little the better to get more. By showing that we deserve the little is the best way to gain much. Once in the United States uniform, the colored man has a springing board under him by which he can jump to loftier heights."[47]

Fifty thousand blacks had enlisted in the Union Army by the end of 1863.[48]

By that time it became apparent after colored troops saw actions at Port Hudson, Milliken's Bend, Mound Plantation and Battery Wagner that the perception the blacks could not and would not fight had been overturned. The colored troops in these battles fought with distinction and with great bravery.[49]

By June, 1864, the War Department had been bombarded by questions concerning the use of colored

---

[45] Publication Number M-1821, pg. 2

[46] The Negro's Civil War, pg. 181

[47] Ibid, pg. 177

[48] African American Soldier in the Civil War, USCT 1862-66, pg. 6

[49] Black Soldiers in Blue, pg. 46

troops. Some regiments of USCT were totally being used for fatigue or garrison duty. The commanders in the field demanded a directive as to whether they were allowed to use the USCT as actual soldiers in battle.

On June 15, 1864, the War Department finally clarified the problem by issuing the following directive: "The incorporation into the Army of the United States of colored troops, renders it necessary that they be brought as speedily as possible into the highest state of discipline. Accordingly the practice which hitherto prevailed, no doubt from necessity, of requiring these troops to perform most of the labor of fortifications, and the labor and fatigue duties of permanent stations and camps, will cease, and they will only be required to take their fair share of fatigue duties with white troops. This is necessary to prepare them for higher duties of conflict with the enemy."[50]

President Lincoln commented on the contributions of the USCT in a letter dated September 12, 1864. He said, "We cannot spare the hundred and forty or fifty thousand now serving us as soldiers, seamen, and laborers. This is not a question of sentiment or taste, but one of physical force which may be measured and estimated as horse-power and steam-power are measured and estimated. Keep it and you can save the Union. Throw it away and the Union goes with it."[51]

By October 20, 1864, there were 101,950 colored soldiers in one hundred and forty Negro regiments in service of the Union. By that same time, there were six colored cavalry regiments. The 3rd U.S. Cavalry was made up entirely of freed men from Mississippi and Tennessee.[52]

All the black regiments, except for Butler's native Guards in Louisiana, had white officers.[53] White soldiers could take leave from their regiment to study at the

---

[50] The Negro's Civil War, pg. 196
[51] Ibid, pg. 235
[52] Ibid, pg. 223
[53] African American Soldier in the Civil War, USCT 1862-66, pg. 6

preparatory academy in Philadelphia for a chance to become an officer in the USCT.[54] The Free Military School, founded by Colonel John H. Taggert, operated on Chestnut Street in Philadelphia from December 26, 1863 until September 15, 1864. Its stated purpose was to train white officers for commands in the USCT.[55]

Many of the colored soldiers were uneducated and others had never fired a weapon. But they were determined to learn. And their white offers drilled them hard.[56]

In the beginning, most people seriously expected that the colored soldiers would not fight. It was also believed that they could not be trusted in a conflict. That was the perception from white soldiers who were from both Union and Confederacy. By the end of the bloody conflict, it was known instead that the colored troops were "dogged defense, relentless in attack and disciplined when on garrison duty."[57]

---

[54] African American Soldier in the Civil War, USCT 1862-66, pg. 6

[55] United States Colored Troops, 1863-1867, pg. 31

[56] African American Soldier in the Civil War, USCT 1862-66, pgs. 15 & 16

[57] Ibid, pgs. 6 & 7

Pay Discrepancy Controversy

Although promised equal army pay, the black soldiers did not receive equal wages. In the recruitment of colored soldiers, Secretary of War Stanton had promised them equal pay ($13 per month plus $3 for uniform allowance). But War Department solicitor William Whiting proclaimed that under the Militia Act of 1863, blacks would be paid instead the sum of $10 with $3 withheld for uniforms. Those voting for the act had evidently assumed that the colored enlistees would act as laborers and not soldiers. On June 4, 1863, in General Order No. 163, Secretary Stanton confirmed the lower pay. Members of the USCT were quite unhappy about the reversal of pay they had been promised.[58]

The colored soldiers were also denied the bounty many white soldiers received for enlisting. Bounties, often as much as five hundred dollars, were paid by local, state and federal authorities to encourage enlistments. The Commonwealth of Pennsylvania later added a ten dollar bounty for black recruits. Later in 1863, through efforts of the Union league in Philadelphia, a two hundred fifty dollar bounty was paid to colored recruits.[59]

In explaining the 54th Massachusetts and 55th Massachusetts soldiers refusal to accept their pay in protest, Captain Luis Emilio (54th Massachusetts) wrote of the pay discrepancy saying "a more pitiful story of broken faith with attendant want and misery upon dependent ones than this ....cannot be told."[60]

Frederick Douglass criticized the pay differential numerous times. Looking back on the issue after the war, he said: "the employment of colored troops at all was a great gain to the colored people – that the measure could not have

---

[58] Black Soldiers in Blue, pg. 49
[59] Strike a Blow for Freedom, page 17
[60] Black Soldiers in Blue, pg. 49

been successfully adopted at the beginning of the war, that the wisdom of making colored men soldiers was still doubted – that their enlistment was a serious offense to popular prejudice…that the fact that they were not to receive the same pay as white soldiers seemed a necessity to smooth the way to their employment at all as soldiers, but that ultimately they would receive the same."[61]

The colored soldiers were impatient and near mutiny in some regiments with the pay issue lingering throughout the war. The 3rd South Carolina Volunteers, led by Sgt. William Walker, marched to the captain's tent, stacked their guns, and refused to fight. Sgt. Walker insisted that since the government had failed to live up to the contract the men had signed upon enlistment, the soldiers were thereby released from further duty. The action got Sgt. Walker court-martialed and executed.[62]

Corporal Gooding explained the reason the colored Massachusetts regiments refused to accept the lower pay in a letter to the *New Bedford Mercury* as follows: "Too many of our comrades' bones lie bleaching near the walls of Fort Wagner. To subtract even one *cent* from our hard earned pay would rob a whole race from their title to manhood, and, even make them feel, no matter how faithful, how brave they had been, that their mite towards founding liberty on a firm basis was spurned, and made a mock of."[63]

Massachusetts Governor John Andrew attempted to rectify the situation by asking the Massachusetts legislature to fund the difference between what the federal government was paying the colored troops and what the white soldiers were receiving. The legislature passed the proposal but the 54th and 55th Massachusetts soldiers continued to refuse their pay because of the unequal treatment from the federal government.[64]

---

[61] The Negro's Civil War, pg. 197
[62] Black Soldiers in Blue, pg. 51
[63] Ibid, pg. 50
[64] The Negro's Civil War, pg. 197

On September 28, 1863, Corporal Gooding expressed his frustrations and the frustration of the colored troops in a letter to Abraham Lincoln written from Morris Island, South Carolina.

President Abraham Lincoln
Washington
Sept. 28, 1863

"Your Excellency will pardon the presumption of an humble individual like myself, in addressing you, but the earnest Solicitation of my Comrades at Arms, besides the genuine interest felt by myself in the matter is my excuse for placing before the Executive head of the Nation our Common Grievance: On the 6th of the last Month, the Paymaster of the department informed us, that if we would decide to receive the sum of $10 (ten dollars) per month, he would come and pay us that sum, but, that, on sitting of Congress, the Regt. would, in his opinion, be allow the other 3 (three). He did not give us any guarantee that this would be, as he hoped, certainly he had no authority for making any such guarantee, and we can not supose (sic) him acting in any way interested. Now the main question is. Are we Soldiers, or are we LABOURERS? We are fully armed, and equipped, have done all the various Duties, pertaining to Soldiers life, have conducted ourselves, to the complete satisfaction of General Officers, who, were if any, prejudice against us, but who now accord us all the encouragement, and honour due us; have shared the perils, and Labour, of Reducing the first stronghold, that flaunted a Traitor Flag; and more, Mr. President. Today, the Anglo Saxon Mother, Wife or Sister, are not alone, in tears for departed Sons, Husbands and Brothers. The patient Trusting Descendents of

Afics Clime, have dyed the ground with blood, in defense of the Union, and Democracy. Men too your Excellency, who know in a measure, the cruelties of the Iron heel of oppression, which in years gone by, the very Power, their blood is now being spilled to maintain, ever ground them to dust. But When the war trumpet sounded o'er the land, when men knew not the Friend from the Traitor, the Black man laid his life on the Altar of the Nation, and he was refused. When the arms of the union were beaten, in the first year of the war, and the Executive called for more food, for its ravaging maw, again the black man begged, the privilege of Aiding his country in her need, to be again refused. And now, he is in the War, and how has he conducted himself? Let their dusky forms, rise up, out of the mires of James Island, and give the answer. Let the rich mould around Wagners parapets be upturned, and there will be found an Eloquent answer. Obedient and patient, and Solid as a wall are they. All we lack, is a paler hue, and a better acquaintance with the Alphabet. Now Your Excellency, we have done a Soldiers Duty. Why can't we have a Soldier's Pay? You caution the Rebel Chieftain, that the United States knows no distinction in her Soldiers: she insists on having all her Soldiers, or whatever creed or Color, to be treated according to the usages of War. Now if the United States exacts uniformity of treatment of her Soldiers from the insurgents, would it not be well, and consistent, to set the example herself, by paying all her *Soldiers* alike? We of this Regt. were not enlisted under any "contraband" act. But we do not wish to be understood, as rating our service, of more Value to the Government, than the service of the ex-slave. Their Service is undoubtedly worth much to the Nation, but Congress made express provision touching their case, as slaves freed by military necessity, and assuming the Government, to be their temporary Guardian; not so with us Freemen by birth, and consequently, having the advantage of *thinking*, and acting for ourselves, so far as the Laws would allow us. We do not consider ourselves the subjects for the Contraband Act. We appeal to You, Sir; as the Executive of the Nation, to have us Justly Dealt with. The Regt., do pray, that they be assured their service will be fairly appreciated, by paying them as American SOLDIERS, not as menial hirelings. Black men You may know well we are poor, three dollars per month, for a year, will supply their needy Wives and little ones, with fuel. If you, as chief Magistrate of the Nation, will assure us, of our whole pay. We are content, our Patriotism, our enthusiasm will have a new impetus, to exert our energy more to air Our Country. Not that our hearts ever flagged, in Devotion, spite the evident apathy displayed in our behalf, but We feel as though, our Country spurned us, now we are sworn to serve her.

Please give this a moments attention.
James Henry Gooding[65]

Secretary of War Stanton suggested legislation to make the soldiers pay equal in December of 1863 in his annual report to Congress. Thaddeus Steven of Pennsylvania introduced the legislation. Many expected its quick passage, but Democrats argued that equal pay would degrade the white army. Conservative Republicans also opposed the measure and delayed it. [66]

The issue was not resolved until Congress and the President finally approved equal pay on June 15, 1864, but even then they added a qualifier. Black soldiers who had

---

[65] www.learner.org/workshops/primarysources/emancipation/docs/jhgooding.html

[66] The Negro's Civil War, pg. 199

been enslaved at the start of the war would receive retroactive equal pay from January 1, 1864. Those who had been free at the start of the war would receive back pay to their enlistment date plus their bounty payments.[67]

On March 3, 1865, Congress addressed the issue again. This time they granted full retroactive pay to any colored soldier who had been promised equal pay at his enlistment. Several months after that, the War Department authorized the payment of bounties for any colored soldier who enlisted after July 18, 1864 (denying the claims of any slave who enlisted prior to that date).[68]

---

[67] Black Soldiers in Blue, pg. 51
[68] Ibid, pg. 52

USCT action at Olustee, Florida – February 20, 1864

Four USCT regiments were involved at Ocean Pond/Olustee, Florida – the 8th USCT, the 54th Massachusetts, the 35th USCT (1st North Carolina) and the 2nd North Carolina USCT. The 1st North Carolina and the 54th Massachusetts were in a brigade commanded by Colonel James Montgomery.[69] At Olustee, they were commanded by Colonel Edward N. Hallowell who led thirteen officers and four hundred eighty enlisted men.[70]

1st North Carolina (also known as 35th U.S. Colored Troops)

The 1st North Carolina was organized at New Bern, North Carolina and Portsmouth, Virginia and was entered into service on June 30, 1863.[71] Nearly all of the men making up the 1st North Carolina were former slaves.[72]

The 35th USCT regiment had been re-designated and fought in the battle as the 1st North Carolina. Approximately six hundred men from the 1st North Carolina took part in the battle at Olustee.[73]

The 1st North Carolina's losses at Olustee were twenty-two killed, one hundred thirty-one wounded and seventy-seven missing in action.[74]

8th U.S. Colored Troops

The 8th USCT consisted of mostly free blacks from Pennsylvania. They were organized between November and December, 1863 at Camp William Penn, Pennsylvania.[75] They were part of Hawley's brigade and were commanded

---

[69] Black Soldiers in Blue, pg. 138
[70] Ibid
[71] Ibid
[72] Ibid
[73] Ibid
[74] Ibid, pg. 144
[75] Publication Number M-1821, pg. 2

by Colonel Charles I. Fribley, who had twenty-one officers and five hundred forty-four enlisted men in his command at Olustee.[76]

In February, the 8th USCT regiment joined General Gilmore's forces at Olustee, Florida. At the time of their involvement in the battle, the 8th USCT hadn't even finished their basic training.[77] Historian William H. Nulty said of the 8th USCT at Olustee that they were "a completely new and combative-inexperienced unit which had never even practiced firing their weapons…sent into action with weapons empty, to deploy and load their weapons while under fire. It was remarkable that they stayed where they were for an hour and a half."[78]

Of the three colored units at Olustee, the 8th USCT suffered the highest casualties. Their losses were forty-nine killed, one hundred eighty-eight wounded and seventy-three missing in action.[79]

54th Massachusetts U.S. Colored Troops – the regiment made famous by the movie "Glory"

Of the seventy some Massachusetts regiments, two were U.S. Colored Troops – the 54th and 55th Massachusetts. The 54th Massachusetts regiment was raised by William Grace, a white merchant from New Bedford, Massachusetts.[80] They were originally comprised of free blacks from Massachusetts and Pennsylvania.[81]

The 54th Massachusetts Volunteers later included soldiers from twenty-four different states. Only about twenty-five percent had ever been slaves. About half could read and write. Many of the men had been active at James

---

[76] Black Soldiers in Blue, pg. 138

[77] Ibid, pg. 136

[78] Ibid, pg. 56

[79] Ibid, pg. 144

[80] African American Soldier in the Civil War, USCT 1862-66, pg. 10

[81] Black Soldiers in Blue, pg. 138

Island, Honey Hill, Boykins Mill and Fort Wagner in South Carolina in July, 1863. [82]

The 54th Massachusetts Volunteers were the only one of the USCT regiments at Olustee with any battle experience.[83] The 54th Massachusetts Volunteers had about six hundred soldiers at Olustee with losses of thirteen killed, sixty-five wounded and eight missing.[84]

Forty-seven USCT soldiers who were wounded or captured at Olustee including two of their white officers were first taken to Tallahassee for several weeks before they were moved by train, wagon and steamer to Andersonville prison in Georgia.[85]

[82] United States Colored troops, 1863-1867, pg. 27

[83] Black Soldiers in Blue, pg. 138

[84] Ibid, pg. 144

[85] Ibid, pgs. 144 & 145

USCT action at Fort Pillow, a Union garrison on the Mississippi River in April 1864

The fort was guarded by a Union garrison of three hundred men of the 13th Tennessee and three hundred USCT, many from the 6th U.S. Heavy Artillery. They were attacked by a larger Confederate force led by General Nathan Bedford Forrest and after fierce fighting, surrendered.

Following the surrender of the Union forces, Forrest's men, with or without orders, continued to kill the USCT soldiers. Reports of the conflict say that almost eighty percent of the black troops who held the garrison were killed, including some who were killed while trying to lay down their arms and surrender. The massacre became a sore spot in the war. Only sixty two of the three hundred USCT survived. Reports from both sides indicated that the USCT fought bravely, were well trained and preformed equal to any white soldiers in the battle.[86]

---

[86] Black Soldiers in Blue, pg. 43

USCT action at Petersburg, Virginia in July 1864

During the long siege at Petersburg, Union soldiers from Pennsylvania coal mining areas dug a tunnel under the Confederate lines. The idea was to fill the tunnel with explosives and blow it up, allowing the Union soldiers to come up behind Confederate lines.

USCT soldiers were trained to go through the tunnel and knew what to do when they came out the other side. At the last minute, Union generals argued that the USCT men could not be trusted with the assignment and white troops were substituted but not trained for the attack. When the explosion went off on July 30, 1864 – white troops were slaughtered coming out of the tunnel. The incident (also sometimes called the Battle of the Crater) was a disaster.[87]

The 4th division of the Ninth Corps, Brigadier General Edward Ferrero's USCT suffered many casualties in the battle, including colored men killed while trying to surrender.[88]

---

[87] African American Soldiers in the Civil War, pg. 54
[88] Strike a Blow for Freedom, pg. 59

By War's End

The Tribune, New Orleans, Sept. 20, 1864

...Still there was a black spot on the National escutcheon, which, fostering and gangrening, kept pace with the growth of the country. Six hundred thousand slaves in 1790 increased in 1860 to four million. A peculiar institution had fastened itself and though opposed to every political principle upon which the Federal System was founded, it defied every effort of the people either to modify, or abolish it. Entrenched behind the Constitution, its upholders and apologists badly held the reins of government; and allying themselves with the party of Progress, adopting the principle of rule, or reign they determined to destroy the Union, or destroy themselves. Profiting by the election of a minority candidate for Presidency, they rushed the slave holding states into revolution, inaugurated civil war, embarked in an attempt to subvert the Union, initiated a reign of terror throughout the South and brought about the present condition of things....

It was quite natural for all the people who were attached to the Union and who were not interested in the ownership of slaves to see in the early stages of the rebellion the speedy destruction of the entire system. Its utter compatibility with free government was made manifest by the war; and though ministering perhaps to the physical growth and prosperity of the Free States, it was opposed to every correct principle of social and political relations, and only served to retard the slave states in their development and progress. Such was the rapid rise of these opinions that they soon spread over the entire country. Even under what was called the "War Power" of the Executive, those opposed to the institution soon found in the Constitution itself, the means for its destruction; and a timid President, waiting sterilely attendant upon public opinion instead of bravely leading it, after many haltings and delays, at last launched his Proclamation of Emancipation, and virtually, by this dilatory step, with which a Jackson would have begun a war, ended it. For, ever since then, the fate of the rebellion, so far as the contests at arms was concerned, has been doubly and trebly assured. Two hundred thousand black soldiers are now in the National armies. No longer under the stars and stripes is the expression of an opinion hostile to slavery punished by hanging, tar, and feathers, rolling in bales, social tabooing, or the trial and imprisonment prescribed by Louisiana statutes. We are fortunately free now, even while still under all the restraints of martial law, to proclaim slavery both a curse and a sin, even from the housetops.

If then it be asked, restore us to "the Union as it was," the manifest reply is that is impossible, for how could such a Union be brought about. Could you say to the 200,000 black soldiers, good, gentle, quiet, patient, docile creatures, do for the sake of the Union of white men, return to your owners and be again slaves! Give them your labor for their husks! Cower down into slaves, and sacrifice yourselves for the benefit of the Oligarchy such as the world has never before seen or felt! We think even a slaveholder would hesitate in making such a preposterous request; and that even he, with all his foolish notion of the "divine institution" and of the inferiority and stupidity of the colored men would know the certain answer he would receive...They must have free speech, free schools, free press, free religion, free government, free individual development, for each of these is as indispensable to their existence as free air...[89]

The Colored Tennessean, Nashville, March 24, 1866
...We are no lovers of hero worship, neither do we believe in defying anything human; but we *do* believe that those men who went into the field to put down treason and rebellion have earned at least the poor compensation of their country's gratitude. To say that the colored troops did not do much towards subjugating the rebels is to say that they, the rebels themselves do not believe. It is even probable that the war would have been yet on the government's hands and had it not been for our black soldiers.[90]

By the end of the war, 179,975 colored soldiers had served in the Union forces, which included one hundred and thirty five infantry regiments, six cavalry regiments, twelve heavy artillery regiments, and ten light artillery batteries. An additional 9,695 served in the U.S. Navy. Less than one sixth of the colored Union soldiers were from free states. Colored Union enlistments from Tennessee, Mississippi and Louisiana alone numbered 99,337.[91] The USCT soldiers appeared in four hundred and forty-nine engagements, including thirty-nine major battles.[92]

About one in five colored soldiers died of disease. That compares to just one in twelve white soldiers.[93] Of the 68,178 black soldiers who died in the war, only 2,751 were killed in action.[94]

---

[89] The Black Press, pg. 88
[90] Ibid, pg. 91
[91] African American Soldier in the Civil War, USCT 1862-66, pg. 9
[92] Men of Color, pg. 4 and Black Soldiers in Blue, pg. 52
[93] Black Soldiers in Blue, pg. 41
[94] Ibid

Seventeen colored soldiers and four colored sailors received the Congressional Medal of Honor.[95] Not more than one hundred colored soldiers and sailors received officer's commissions during the entire war.[96]

By the end of the war, General Benjamin Butler commanded the Army of the James comprised of the 25th Corps, which was unique in that it was the first and only U.S. Army Corps made up completely of U. S. colored soldiers.[97]

The last regiment of USCT soldiers was mustered out of federal service in December, 1867.[98]

---

[95] The Negro's Civil War, pg. 237

[96] Ibid, pg. 239

[97] Black Soldiers in Blue, pg. 22

[98] Publication Number M-1821, pg. 2

U.S. Colored troops in Confederate prisons

There were seven hundred and seventy-six colored soldiers in Confederate prisons including Andersonville, Salisbury, Danville and Libby prisons.[99] It is possible that some of these men were counted more than once. Twelve soldiers from the 54th Massachusetts who were prisoners from Andersonville prison were transferred to the prison in Florence, South Carolina. Several USCT from Andersonville prison were released from Salisbury or Danville prisons in North Carolina. Many of the prisoners from Libby prison were transferred to Andersonville.

Most USCT soldiers when captured were killed. Even if they were taken to a Confederate prison, they rarely received any medical help. The USCT men knew they would not be exchanged because the Confederates didn't have many colored troops to exchange.

A total of two hundred eighty-four USCT soldiers reportedly died in Confederate prisoner of war camps. Over ten percent of those deaths were at Andersonville Prison. Additionally there were two hundred thirty-six colored prisoners who were exchanged and seventy-seven who escaped from various prisons.[100]

[99] United States Colored Troops, 1863-1867, pg. 97
[100] Men of Color, pg. 118

Andersonville Prison

The stockade at Andersonville, Georgia (known as Camp Sumter or Andersonville Prison) was an enclosure of approximately twenty-six and a half acres surrounded by a fifteen foot high fence. The wall surrounded the ground where the prisoners sat was 750 feet long on the ends and 1540 feet long on the sides.

The prison received its first Union prisoners on February 24, 1864. It had no sanitary facilities or housing. A creek ran through the stockade but was polluted by human wastes. Guard positions (about fifty in total) were placed along spots on the wall where sentries watched those incarcerated within the enclosure.

The facility, originally built to hold 6,000 prisoners, held 45,613 Union soldiers during the fourteen months it was open.

Supplies, including food and medicine were scarce. Thousands died in the enclosure. By the summer of 1864, more than one hundred men died every single day.[101] A total of 12,912 died in the Andersonville prison.[102]

Note – For a more complete look at the Andersonville Prison, please see "Andersonville", by MacKinlay Kantor, The World Publishing Company, Cleveland and New York, 1955; "A Captive of War", by Solon Hyde, Burd Street Press, Shippensburg, Pennsylvania, originally published in 1900; "Andersonville Diary", by John L. Ransom, Digital Scanning Inc., Scituate, Massachusetts, originally published in 1881; and "Catesby: Eyewitness to the Civil War", by Bob O'Connor, Infinity Publishing, West Conshohocken, Pennsylvania, 2008.

---

[101] Andersonville, Georgia USA, pgs. 9 & 10
[102] Andersonville Diary, pg. 287

USCT soldiers held prisoner at Andersonville Prison

One hundred and three of a total of over 45,000 Union prisoners at Andersonville Prison were USCT men. Of the one hundred three USCT prisoners, forty-seven had been captured at the battle of Olustee.

The treatment of the USCT prisoners at Andersonville was chronicled by Private Robert Knox Sneden of the 40th New York Volunteers who was also a prisoner at Andersonville. In his diary, Sneden observed, "a dozen or more Negroes, all prisoners of war. Nearly all minus an arm or leg, and their wounds are yet unhealed. Many of them are gangrened and they will all surely die. They keep by themselves and are very quiet. The Rebels have removed every vestige of any uniform they once wore, and then have nothing on but old cast off jean jackets and cotton shirts. All are bareheaded and barefooted, and thin as skeletons. Those captured who were able to work are kept at work outside by the Rebels, felling trees, making roads, etc., etc. Their officers have been made to eat and sleep with Negroes."[103]

Of all the USCT enlisted men at Andersonville prison, most is known about Corporal James Gooding of the 54th Massachusetts (as already mentioned above in the disputed pay section) and white officer Archibald Bogle of the 1st North Carolina (35th USCT). Ironically, both were listed in their local newspapers as having died in action at Olustee. Obviously Bogle and Gooding both survived that battle. Their two obituaries are listed first.

---

[103] Black Soldiers in Blue, pg. 49

Corporal James Gooding – 54th Massachusetts Volunteers – USCT – Obituary and information

New Bedford Mercury, March 9, 1864
Jacksonville, Florida, February 25, 1864

Messrs. Editor: I am pained to inform you that Corporal James H. Gooding was killed in battle on the 20th inst. at Olustee Station.[104] He was one of the Color (sic) Corporals and was with the colors (sic) at the time. So great was the rout of our troops that we left nearly all our dead and wounded on the field. The fight lasted four hours. We were badly beaten that night, and the next day we kept falling back, until we reached Jacksonville. The fifty-fourth did honor to themselves and our city. All concede that no regiment fought like it.

James H Buchanan, of New Bedford, was killed; and Sergeant Wharton A. Williams, also of our city, was wounded in the hand. Many others of Company C were wounded; but none of them from our city.

The regiment is pleased to learn that the bill to pay them $13 per month passed.

The total loss of the regiment, I am unable to give to you at this time. All we want now is more troops; with them we would go forward again and drive the rebels from the State.

Your Friend, James W. Grace, Captain Fifty-fourth Regiment (Massachusetts)[105]

Corporal James Henry Gooding was married to Ellen Louisa Allen of New Bedford, Massachusetts on September

---

[104] Actually Gooding was wounded in the thigh and captured at Olustee and taken to Andersonville Prison.
www.battleofolustee.org/letters/grace.html
[105] www.battleofolustee.org/letters/grace.html

28, 1862. Their marriage did not produce children. Gooding was five feet five and a half inches tall, had brown skin and curly hair, with black eyes. In 1856 at the age of 18 he signed on as a whaler on the crew ship *Sunbeam*.[106]

Gooding was educated and left letters to indicate how he and his fellow soldiers in the 54th Massachusetts felt about several issues of their soldiering days. He wrote in the summer of 1862 that "there is not a man in the regiment who does not appreciate the difficulties, the dangers, and maybe ignoble death that awaits him, if captured by a foe, and they will die upon the field rather than be hanged like a dog."[107]

Major Archibald Bogle – 1st North Carolina (35th USCT) – Obituary and information

Boston Journal, March 2, 1864
1st North Carolina Colored Infantry

Death of Major Archibald Bogle, 1st Regiment North Carolina Colored Infantry. The sad news reached this city yesterday that Major Bogle of the 1st North Carolina Colored Infantry had been killed in the late battle (Olustee) in Florida. Upon his relatives and friends the intelligence fell with distressing weight. Major Bogle was the only son of Wm. Bogle, Esq., of Melrose.

He was formerly a member of the 2nd Battalion M.W.M, and did duty at Fort Warren during the time the Battalion was stationed there in 1861. He was afterwards commissioned 2nd Lieutenant in the 17th Regiment Mass. Volunteers, and left the Commonwealth, never to return, August 25, 1861. He was afterward promoted 1st Lieutenant in the 17th, a position he held until he was selected by Brigadier General Wild of the 1st

---

[106] Ibid
[107] Black Soldiers in Blue, pg. 40

Regiment of colored infantry, raised in North Carolina.[108]

Major Bogle was one of the promising young officers that left Massachusetts during this war. Although but 22 years of age, he was complete master of his profession. He had a natural adaptation for military study and science. His temperament was remarkably cool and steady. He was never excited, and never lost his poise.

A braver and truer heart never beat under a soldier's uniform. He fell at the head of his regiment, far from home, and kindred, but his memory will be ever cherished with warm affection by all who knew him as a brave, good man who gave up his young life on the battle field of his country and humanity.[109]

During battle of Olustee, on February 20, 1864, Major Archibald Bogle of the 1st North Carolina Infantry (35th USCT) was injured and removed to the rear. He suffered from a broken leg and a chest wound. He was captured by the Confederates and was taken by train to Camp Sumter, (Andersonville Prison) Andersonville, Georgia.[110]

Major Bogle arrived at Andersonville Prison on March 14, 1864, carried on a litter by soldiers who had been captured with him. Although he was an officer, the Confederates refused to acknowledge him because he was a white officer of the USCT. In spite of his wound, the medical staff would not treat him.[111]

---

[108] Official records indicate that Bogle was promoted for gallant conduct on the field in May 1862 and was promoted to major in the 35th USCT in May 1863. www.battleofolustee.org/letters/1stnc-1.htm

[109] Obviously the obituary was in error, as Major Bogle did not die at Olustee, but was captured and sent to Andersonville prison. www.battleofolustee.org/letters/1stnc-1.htm

[110] www.battleofolustee.org/letters/bogle.htm

[111] Ibid

Although hobbling on crutches and wounded in the bowel, Major Bogle was refused medical treatment at the prison hospital. The other U.S. Colored troops were also refused medical assistance.

On November 18, 1864, Major Bogle and seven other prisoners were transferred to the Camp Lawton Prisoner of War Camp in Millen, Georgia.[112] Major Bogle was finally paroled at Wilmington, North Carolina in March, 1865. He was discharged in April, 1866 at Charleston, South Carolina.

On May 21, 1867, Bogle was appointed 1st Lieutenant in the 39th Infantry. He served with his company in New Orleans up to January 1868 and at Fort Pike, Louisiana to March 1869. On April 20, 1869, he was transferred to the 25th Infantry where he served at Baton Rogue, LA; Ship Island, MS; Jackson Barracks, LA; Memphis, TN; and Duncan, TX.

Major Bogle remained in the service with his final discharge on December 20, 1871. On that same day Court Martial Order 29 was issued against 1st Lt. Archibald Bogle. The order charged Lt. Bogle with two counts resulting from an incident at Fort Duncan, TX. Lt. Bogle was charged with conduct unbecoming of an officer as he allegedly shot a pistol at Assistant Surgeon Alfred C. Girard, and with assault with intent to kill, to the prejudice good order and military discipline. The president of the court was Colonel Abner Doubleday. Lt. Bogle was found guilty on both counts, and was sentenced to be discharged from the service and to be confined for two years in a penitentiary. The court then agreed to recommend "in consideration of the previous good character and excellent record of the accused during the later rebellion, so much of the sentence related to confinement in a penitentiary be remitted."

---

[112] Camp Lawton was built in September 1864 to relieve crowding at Andersonville Prison. The first prisoner arrived in October – with the number of prisoners on hand by November estimated to be 10,299. On November 24, 1864 the camp was abandoned and the prisoners moved due to General Sherman's advancing army.
www.mycivilwar.com/pow/ga-millen.htm

The recommendation was approved by the War Department due to the fact that no one was injured in the incident and of Lt. Bogle's previous confinement in Andersonville Prison. [113]

Archibald Bogle died in Oakland, California on October 22, 1893. His birthplace is listed on the death certificate as Scotland. He was 53 years old when he died. He had been married for 35 years to Anna Conover. His death certificate states his cause of death as "alcoholic cirrhosis of the liver." Statements by physicians who treated him during the latter stages of his life said he died of "malarial condition of the liver" and "bowels obstructed caused by a stricture from a gunshot wound received in service in the Civil War."[114]

---

[113] www.battleofolustee.org/letters/bogle.htm
[114] www.battleofolustee.org/letters/1stnc-1.htm

The two white officers of the USCT at Andersonville Prison

Major Archibald Bogle (see pgs. 35 - 38)

Lt. Colonel George French, 8th USCT, also captured at Olustee, Florida.

Both Bogle and French should have been placed with the Union officers at a nearby stockade, but were imprisoned with the enlisted men due to their affiliation with the USCT soldiers.

Major Bogle being the highest ranking officer of the USCT at Andersonville Prison became the commanding officer of those USCT confined in the prison.

Major Bogle survived Andersonville Prison. Lt. Colonel French died in the prison.

The USCT prisoners at Andersonville Prison - Chart

Regiment	# of prisoners	survivors	deaths
2nd North Carolina	1	0	1
8th USCT (Pennsylvania)	34	14	20
16th USCT (Tennessee)	1	0	1
17th USCT	1	0	1
18th USCT	1	0	1
30th Connecticut	1	0	1
35th USCT (1st North Carolina)	6	2	4
45th USCT	1	1	0
54th Massachusetts	53	48	5
137th USCT	4	4	0
Totals	**103**	**69**	**34**

List of the deceased U. S. Colored soldiers at Andersonville

Irving Hall (listed as J. Hall in prison records) 8th U.S. Colored Troops, Private, Company E – Mustered in 8-14-1863 – Captured at Olustee, Florida on 2-20-1864 – Died 4-24-1864 – Cause of death, Diarrhea C. – Grave # 711[115]

---

[115].www.angelfire.com/ga4/usct/8thusct.html, Andersonville Records # 10711, Andersonville Diary, pg. 261 and The History of the Pennsylvania Volunteers, 1861-1865, Vol. V., pg. 978

Howell Turnace (also listed as Turner/Yurner), 2nd North Carolina (also listed as 1st N. C./35th USCT), Private, Company I – Muster date unknown – Captured at Olustee, Florida on 2-20-1864 – Died 4-29-1864 – Cause of death, Diarrhea C. – Grave # 798[116]

[116] www.angelfire.com/ga4/usct/8thusct.html, Andersonville Records # 10798 and Andersonville Diary, pg. 248

Wilson Briggs, 35th U. S. Colored Troops (1st North Carolina), Company A – Muster and capture information unknown – Died 5-3-1864 – Grave # 849[117]

[117] Andersonville Diary, pg. 248

Clement Shilton (Shelton), 8th U.S. Colored Troops, Private, Company I – Mustered in 8-28-1863 – Captured at Olustee, Florida on 2-20-1864 – Died 5-20-1864 – Cause of death, Diarrhea – Grave # 1236[118]

[118] www.angelfire.com/ga4/usct/8thusct.html, Andersonville Records # 11236 and Andersonville Diary, pg. 284

George H. Burton, Substitute, 18th U.S. Colored Troops (also listed as 8th USCT), Private, Company I – Captured at Olustee, Florida on 2-20-1864 – Died 5-21-1864 – Cause of death, Diarrhea – Grave # 1266[119]

---

[119] Andersonville Records # 11266, Andersonville Diary, pg. 281, and www.pa-roots.com/pacw/usct/8thUSCTcoa.html

Charles Rensellear (also listed as Rensellar and Rensenlear), 54th Massachusetts Volunteers, Private, Company C – East Hampton, Massachusetts – 21 – Blacksmith – Enlisted on 11-16-1863 – Captured at Olustee, Florida on 2-20-1864 – Died 6-8-1864 – Cause of death, Dysentery – Grave # 1725 [120]

[120] Massachusetts Soldiers, Sailors, and Marines in the Civil War, Vol. IV, pg. 673, Men of Color, pg. 36 and Andersonville Prison Records # 11725

Henry Gardner (also listed as N. Gardiner), 8th U.S. Colored Troops, Company F or H – Mustered in 9-1-1863 – Captured at Olustee, Florida on 2-20-1864 – Died 6-10-1884 – Cause of death, Diarrhea – Grave # 1793[121]

---

[121] Andersonville Records # 11793 and Andersonville Diary, pg. 260

Henry Miller, 8th USCT Cavalry, Company B – Muster and capture information unknown – Died 6-13-1864 – Cause of death unknown – Grave # 1907[122]

---

[122] Andersonville Records # 11907 and Andersonville Diary, pg. 264

William J. Smith, 54th Massachusetts Volunteers, Private, Company K – Salem, Ohio – 24 – Laborer – Enlisted on 5-13-1863 – Captured at Olustee, Florida on 2-20-1864 – Died 6-22-1864 – Cause of death, Dysentery – Grave # 2304[123]

---

[123] Massachusetts Soldiers, Sailors, and Marines in the Civil War, Vol. IV, pg. 709, Andersonville Prison Records # 12304, Men of Color pg. 36, and Andersonville Diary, pg. 219

Mark D. Babcock (listed as R. Babcock), 30th Connecticut, Company A – Muster and capture information unknown -- Died 7-1-1864 – Cause of death, Scorbutus (Scorbutus is death from scurvy resulting most often from lack of Vitamin C in the diet.) – Grave # 2720[124]

---

[124] Andersonville Prison Records # 12720, Records and Service of the Connecticut Men, pg. 885 and Dedication of the Monument at Andersonville, pg. 58

Alexander Whittaker (also listed as Whitaker), 8th U.S. Colored Troops, Private, Co. D – Mustered in 10-13-1863 – Captured at Olustee, Florida on 2-20-1864 – Died 7-2-1864 – Cause of Death, Diarrhea – Grave # 2790[125]

[125] www.angelfire.com/ga4/usct/8thusct.html, Andersonville Records # 12790, The History of the Pennsylvania Volunteers, 1861-1865, Vol. V., pg. 977 and Andersonville Diary, pg. 268

William Scott, 8th U.S. Colored Troops, Private, Company D – Mustered in 8-14-1863 – Captured at Olustee, Florida on 2-20-1864 – Died 7-4-1864 – Cause of death, Diarrhea – Grave # 2864[126]

[126] www.angelfire.com/ga4/usct/8thusct.html, Andersonville Prison Records # 12864, The History of the Pennsylvania Volunteers, 1861-1865, Vol. V., pg. 977 and Andersonville Diary, pg. 267

Lt. Colonel George French – white officer – 8th U.S. Colored Troops (listed also as 37th USCT) – Mustered in 1-21-1863 – 24 – Captured at Olustee, Florida on 2-20-1864 – Died 7-3-1864 (other records indicate death on 7-4) – Cause of death, Fever Remittent – Grave # 2888[127]

[127] Andersonville Records # 12888, The History of the Pennsylvania Volunteers, 1861-1865, Vol. V., pg 984 and Andersonville Diary, pg. 282

James Gooding, 54th Massachusetts, Corporal, Company C – New Bedford, Massachusetts – 26 – Seaman – Enlisted 2-14-1863 (also listed as 3-30-1863) – Captured at Olustee, Florida on 2-20-1864 – Died 7-19-1864 – Cause of death, Wounds – Grave # 3585 [128]

[128] *Massachusetts Soldiers, Sailors, and Marines in the Civil War*, Vol. IV, pg. 671, *Men of Color*, pg. 36, *Andersonville Prison Records* # 13585 and *Andersonville Diary*, pg. 216

William Hopkins, 17th U.S. Colored Troops, Private, Company C – Muster and capture information unknown – Died 7-24-1864 – Cause of death, Anasarca (Anasarca is edema, caused by general kidney or heart failure) – Grave # 3893[129]

---

[129] www.angelfire.com/ga4/usct/17thusct.html, Andersonville Prison Records # 13893 and Andersonville Diary, pg. 282

D. L. Hill (listed as D. S. Hill), 16th U.S. Colored Troops, Company C – Muster date unknown – Captured at Olustee, Florida on 2-20-1864 – Died 7-31-1864 – Cause of death, Diarrhea – Grave # 4429[130]

[130] www.angelfire.com/ga4/usct/16thusct.html, Andersonville Prison Records # 14429 and Andersonville Diary, pg. 282

Jacob Hollingsworth, (Marker says Isaac) 8th U.S. Colored Troops, Private, Company A – Mustered in 7-14-1863 – Captured at Olustee, Florida on 2-20-1864 – Died 8-22-1864 – Cause of death, Diarrhea – Grave # 6481[131]

---

[131] www.angelfire.com/ga4/usct/8thusct.html, Andersonville Prison Records # 16481, The History of the Pennsylvania Volunteers, 1861-1865, Vol. V., pg. 970 and Andersonville Diary, pg. 261

Daniel Phillips (listed as Felps), 8th U.S. Colored Troops, Private, Company H – Mustered in 9-2-1863 – Capture information unknown – Died 8-25-1864 – Cause of death, Diarrhea --Grave # 6804[132]

[132]Andersonville Prison Records # 16804 and Andersonville Diary, pg. 282

William Edwards, 8th U.S. Colored Troops, Sgt., Company A – Mustered in 6-8-1863 (also listed as 9-18-1863) – Captured at Olustee, Florida on 2-20-1864 – Died 8-25-1864 – Cause of death, Diarrhea – Grave # 6813[133]

[133] www.angelfire.com/ga4/usct/8thusct.html, Andersonville Prison Records # 16813, The History of the Pennsylvania Volunteers, 1861-1865, Vol. V., pg. 969 and Andersonville Diary, pg. 282

William Moyer (also listed as Mayer), 8th U.S. Colored Troops Cavalry, Company C – Muster date and capture place unknown – Capture date 5-19-1864 – Died 9-15-1864 – Cause of death, Diarrhea – Grave # 7875[134]

---

[134] Andersonville Prison Records # 17875 and Andersonville Diary, pg. 264

Stephen Thomas, 8th U.S. Colored Troops, Private, Company D – Mustered in 8-15-1863 – Captured at Olustee, Florida on 2-20-1864 – Died 9-9-1864 – Cause of death, Fever intermittent – Grave # 8279[135]

[135] www.angelfire.com/ga4/usct/8thusct.html, Andersonville Prison Records # 18279, The History of the Pennsylvania Volunteers, 1861-1865, Vol. V., pg. 977 and Andersonville Diary, pg. 284

Charles August (grave stone says Charles Augustus), 54th Massachusetts Volunteers, Corporal, Company I – Ypsilanti, Michigan – 30 – Blacksmith – Enlisted 4-23-1863 (or 4-13-1863) – Captured at Olustee, Florida on 2-20-1864 (prison records indicate he was captured at Fort Wagner, South Carolina, 7-18-1863) – Died 9-10-1864 – Cause of death, Scorbutus – Grave # 8373[136]

---

[136] Massachusetts Soldiers, Sailors, and Marines in the Civil War, Vol. IV, pg. 700, Andersonville Prison Records # 18373 and Andersonville Diary pg. 215 (listed under Analstine)

William Van Alstine (listed in prison records as Analstine) – 54th Massachusetts Volunteers, Private, Company C – Troy, New York – 19 – Farmer – Enlisted 3-18-1863 – Captured at Fort Wagner, South Carolina on 7-18-1863 – Died 9-10-1864[137]

---

[137] Massachusetts Soldiers, Sailors and Marines in the Civil War, Vol. IV., pg. 674 and Andersonville Prison Records # 30456

Warren Norfelt (also listed as Norflet/Norfield), 35th U. S. Colored Troops (1st North Carolina), Private, Company G – Muster date unknown – Captured at Olustee, Florida on 2-20-1864 – Died on 9-14-1864 – Cause of death, Diarrhea – Grave # 8690[138]

---

[138] www.angelfire.com/ga4/usct/35thusct.html, Andersonville Prison Records # 18690 and Andersonville Diary, pg. 248

William Hooker, 8th U.S. Colored Troops, Company G (also listed as 1st Massachusetts, Company B) – Muster and capture dates unknown – Died 9-18-1864 – Cause of death unknown – Grave # 9118[139]

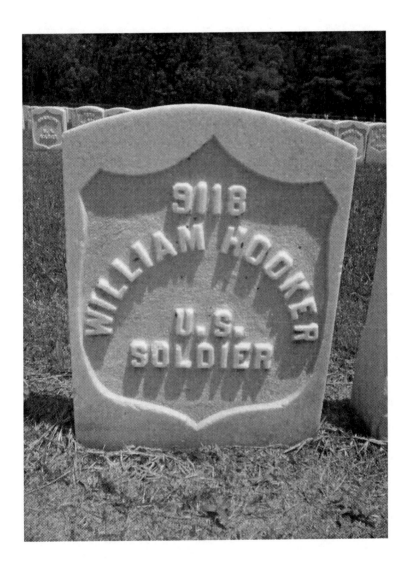

---

[139] Andersonville Prison Records # 19118 and Andersonville Diary, pg. 262

Samuel White, 8th U.S. Colored Troops, Private, Company F – Mustered in 8-14-1863 – Captured at Olustee, Florida on 2-20-1864 – Died 9-18-1864 – Cause of death, Diarrhea – Grave # 9131[140]

---

[140] www.angelfire.com/ga4/usct/8thusct.html, Andersonville Prison Records #19131, The History of the Pennsylvania Volunteers, 1861-1865, Vol. V., pg. 982 and Andersonville Diary, pg. 284

James (also listed as Jno) Walker, 8th U.S. Colored Troops, Private, Company F – Mustered in 10-12-1863 – Captured at Olustee, Florida on 2-20-1864 – Died 9-24-1864 – Cause of death, Diarrhea (also listed as Scorbutus) – Grave # 9677[141]

---

[141] www.angelfire.com/ga4/usct/8thusct.html, Andersonville Prison Records # 19677, Andersonville Diary, pg. 284 and The History of the Pennsylvania Volunteers, 1861-1865, Vol. V., pg. 982

Samuels Waters, 8th U.S. Colored Troops, Sgt., Company C – Muster date unknown – Captured at Olustee, Florida on 2-20-1864 – Died 10-5-1864 – Cause of death, Diarrhea – Grave # 10374[142]

---

[142] www.angelfire.com/ga4/usct/8thusct.html, Andersonville Prison Records # 20374, The History of the Pennsylvania Volunteers, 1861-1865, Vol. V., pg. 973, The Negro in the American Rebellion, pg. 221 and Andersonville Diary, pg. 284

Harrison Lockwood, 8th U.S. Colored Troops, Private, Company D – Mustered in 9-28-1863 – Captured at Olustee, Florida on 2-20-1864 – Died 10-5-1864 – Cause of death, Diarrhea – Grave # 10379[143]

[143] www.angelfire.com/ga4/usct/8thusct.html, Andersonville Prison Records # 20379, The History of the Pennsylvania Volunteers, 1861-1865, Vol. V., pg. 976 and Andersonville Diary, pg. 283

James Smith, 8th U.S. Colored Troops, Private, Company D – Muster date unknown – Captured at Olustee, Florida on 2-20-1864 – Died on 10-22-1864 – Cause of death, Scorbutus – Grave # 11301[144]

[144] www.angelfire.com/ga4/usct/8thusct.html, Andersonville Prison Records # 21301 and Andersonville Diary, pg. 284

Charles Annon (also listed as Annis and Amon), 8th U.S. Colored Troops, Private, Company I – Mustered in 11-16-1863 – Captured at Olustee, Florida on 2-20-1864 – Died 10-26-1864 – Cause of death, Scorbutus – Grave # 11523[145]

---

[145] www.angelfire.com/ga4/usct/8thusct.html, Andersonville Prison Records # 21523 and Andersonville Diary, pg. 281

William Moss, 35th U. S. Colored Troops (1st North Carolina), Company F – Muster date unknown --Captured at Olustee, Florida on 2-20-1864 – Died 11-5-1864 – Cause of death unknown – Grave # 11844[146]

[146] Andersonville Prison Records # 21844 and Andersonville Diary, pg, 248

William P. Lewis, 8th U.S. Colored Troops, Private, Company B – Mustered in 7-25-1863 – Captured at Olustee, Florida on 2-20-1864 – Died 11-12-1864 – Cause of death, Scorbutus – Grave # 11973[147]

---

[147] www.angelfire.com/ga4/usct/8thusct.html, The History of the Pennsylvania Volunteers, 1861-1865, Vol. V., pg. 973, Andersonville Prison Records # 21973 and Andersonville Diary, pg. 283

E. Hort (also listed as Horst and Holt), 35th U.S. Colored Troops, Company H – Muster date unknown – Captured at Olustee, Florida on 2-20-1864 – Died 2-6-1865 – Cause of death, Diarrhea C. – Grave # 12601[148]

[148] www.angelfire.com/ga4/usct/35thusct.html, Andersonville Prison Records # 22601 and Andersonville Diary, pg. 283

The U.S. Colored Troops who survived Andersonville Prison

- o **Major Archibald Bogle** – white officer of the 35th U.S. Colored Troops – Paroled on 3-1-1865[149] (See pages 35 - 38)

- **8th U.S. Colored Troops**

  - o **Paul Blackman**, Private, Company G – Mustered in 8-19-1863 – Captured at Olustee, Florida on 2-20-1864 – Sick at muster out on 11-10-1865[150]

  - o **George Brown**, Private, Company C – Mustered in 8-13-1863 – Captured at Olustee, Florida on 2-20-1864 – Died at Fortress Monroe on 8-16-1865[151]

  - o **Richard Chancellor**, Private, Company B – Mustered in 6-24-1863 (also listed as 7-21-1863) – Captured at Olustee, Florida on 2-20-1864 – Discharged from service on or about 7-15-1865[152]

  - o **John Fisher**, Private, Company B – Mustered in 6-24-1863 (also listed as 9-24-1863) – Captured at Olustee, Florida on 2-20-1864 – Returned to his regiment on 3-15-1865 – Testified at the trial of Henry Wirz[153]

---

[149] Men of Color, pg. 119
[150] www.angelfire.com/ga4/usct/8thusct.html and Andersonville Prison Records # 41371
[151] www.angelfire.com/ga4/usct/8thusct.html and Andersonville Prison Records # 41363
[152] www.angelfire.com/ga4/usct/8thusct.html and Andersonville Prison Records # 41366
[153] www.angelfire.com/ga4/usct/8thusct.html, The History of the Pennsylvania Volunteers, 1861-1865, Vol. V., pg. 973, Tragedy at Andersonville, The Henry Wirz Trial, The Prison Keeper, pg. 276 and Andersonville Prison Records # 41362

8th USCT (Continued)

- **Joseph Ford**, Private, Company B – Mustered in 8-10-1863 – Captured at Olustee, Florida on 2-20-1864 – Mustered out of service on 11-10-1865[154]

- **Henry Henson**, Private, Company K – Mustered in 11-28-1863 – Captured at Olustee, Florida on 2-20-1864[155]

- **Thomas W. Jackson**, Private Company A – Muster and capture information unknown – Sent to Columbia, South Carolina on 2-2-1865[156]

- **William Henry Jennings**, Private, Company A – Mustered in 9-16-1863 – Captured at Olustee, Florida on 2-20-1864 – Testified at the Henry Wirz Trial[157]

- **George Potter**, Private, Company E – Mustered in 8-29-1863 – Captured at Olustee, Florida on 2-20-1864[158]

- **John Thompson**, Private, Company B – Mustered in 8-14-1863 – Captured at Olustee,

---

[154] www.angelfire.com/ga4/usct/8thusct.html, The History of the Pennsylvania Volunteers, 1861-1865, Vol. V., pg. 972 and Andersonville Prison Records # 41367

[155] www.angelfire.com/ga4/usct/8thusct.html, The History of the Pennsylvania Volunteers, 1861-1865, Vol. V., pg. 989 and Andersonville Prison Records # 41372

[156] www.angelfire.com/ga4/usct/8thusct.html

[157] www.angelfire.com/ga4/usct/8thusct.html and The Tragedy of Andersonville, The Trail of Henry Wirz, The Prison Keeper, pg. 270, The History of the Pennsylvania Volunteers, 1861-1865, Vol. V., pg. 970 and Andersonville Prison Records # 41356

[158] www.angelfire.com/ga4/usct/8thusct.html, The History of the Pennsylvania Volunteers, 1861-1865, Vol. V., pg. 979, and Andersonville Prison Records # 41370

Florida on 2-20-1864 – Paroled on unknown date and died in Baltimore, Maryland[159]

o **Jon Thompson**, Private, Company K – Muster and capture information unknown – Sent to Columbia, South Carolina on 2-28-1865[160]

o **George Washington**, Private, Company E – Mustered in 9-25-1863 – Captured at Olustee, Florida on 2-20-1864 – Sent to Columbia, South Carolina on 2-28-1865 – Testified at the trial of Henry Wirz[161]

o **Abraham Woodruff** (also listed as Woodward), Private, Company H – Mustered in 8-11-1863 – Captured at Olustee, Florida on 2-20-1864 – Discharged from the service on 6-29-1865[162]

o **Molton Young**, Private, Company C – Mustered in 8-13-1863 (also listed as 8-12-1863) – Captured at Olustee, Florida on 2-20-1864[163]

---

[159] www.angelfire.com/ga4/usct/8thusct.html, The History of the Pennsylvania Volunteers, 1861-1865, Vol. V., pg. 973 and Andersonville Prison Records # 41368

[160] www.angelfire.com/ga4/usct/8thusct.html

[161] www.angelfire.com/ga4/usct/8thusct.html, The History of the Pennsylvania Volunteers, 1861-1865, Vol. V., pg. 978, Andersonville Prison Records # 41364 and The Tragedy of Andersonville, The Trial of Henry Wirz, The Prison Keeper, pg. 277

[162] www.angelfire.com/ga4/usct/8thusct.html, The History of the Pennsylvania Volunteers, 1861-1865, Vol. V., pg. 986, The Tragedy of Andersonville, The Henry Wirz Trial, The Prison Keeper, pg. 277 and Andersonville Prison Records # 41365

[163] www.angelfire.com/ga4/usct/8thusct.html, The History of the Pennsylvania Volunteers, 1861-1865, Vol. V., pg. 975 and Andersonville Prison Records # 41369

35th U.S. Colored Troops (1st North Carolina)

- o **Frank Maddox** (also listed as Mattock), Private, Company E – Muster date unknown – Captured at Olustee, Florida on 2-20-1864 – Testified at the trial of Henry Wirz[164]

45th U. S. Colored Troops

- o **John Mackey**[165]

54th Massachusetts Volunteers

- o **James Allen**, Private, Company A – Lafayette, Indiana – 28 – Brakeman – Enlisted May 12, 1862 – Captured at Fort Wagner, South Carolina on 7-18-1863 – Died in prison in Salisbury, North Carolina on 1-18-1865[166]

- o **Solomon E. Anderson** – Company B – West Chester, Pennsylvania – 34 – Farmer -- Enlisted 3-9-1863 (also listed as 3-30-1863) – Captured at Fort Wagner, South Carolina on 7-18-181863 – Died in prison at Florence, South Carolina on 2-22-1865[167]

- o **David Bailey**, Private, Company B – Philadelphia, Pennsylvania – 22 – Laborer Enlisted 2-25-1863 – Captured at Fort Wagner, South Carolina on 7-18-1863 – Died in prison in Florence, South Carolina on or about 1-15-1865[168]

---

[164] www.angelfire.com/ga4/usct/35thusct.html and the Tragedy of Andersonville, The Trial of Henry Wirz, The Prison Keeper, pg. 265 and Andersonville Prison Records # 41354

[165] List of USCT at Andersonville

[166] Massachusetts Soldiers, Sailors, and Marines in the Civil War, Vol. IV, pg. 659 and Andersonville Prison Records # 63156

[167] Massachusetts Soldiers, Sailors, and Marines in the Civil War, Vol. IV, pg. 664 and Andersonville Prison Records # 44606

[168] Andersonville Prison Records # 44607

- **Joseph Bayard**, Private, Company K – Lockport, New York – 28 – Turnkey – Enlisted 5-5-1863 – Captured at Fort Wagner on 7-18-1863 – Exchanged at Goldsboro, North Carolina on March 4, 1865 – Discharged on 9-24-1865 at Dale U.S. General Hospital, Worcester, Massachusetts for disability from wounds [169]

- **Lemuel Blake**, Private, Company B – West Chester, Pennsylvania – 21 – Farmer – Enlisted 3-9-1863 (also listed as 3-30-1863) – Captured at James Island, South Carolina on 7-16-1863 – Exchanged on 3-4-1865 at Goldsboro, North Carolina – Returned to Company on 6-7-1865 – Mustered out 9-20-1865 [170]

- **Jesse H. Brown**, Private, Company B – Unionville, Pennsylvania – 23 – Farmer -- Enlisted 3-11-1863 (also listed as 3-30-1863) – Captured at Fort Wagner, South Carolina on 7-18-1863 – Exchanged on 3-4-1865 at Goldsboro, North Carolina – Returned to Company on 6-8-1865 – Mustered out 9-20-1865 [171]

- **Morris Butler**, Private, Company E – Mt. Holly, New Jersey – 19 – Laborer – Enlisted 4-1-1863 (also listed as 4-23-1863) – Captured at Fort Wagner, South Carolina on 7-18-1863 – Died in prison in Florence, South Carolina 2-12-1865 [172]

---

[169] Massachusetts Soldiers, Sailors, and Marines in the Civil War, Vol. IV, pg. 705 and Andersonville Prison Records # 63389

[170] Massachusetts Soldiers, Sailors, and Marines in the Civil War, Vol. IV, pg. 664 and Andersonville Prison Records # 44608

[171] Massachusetts Soldiers, Sailors, and Marines in the Civil War, Vol. IV, pg. 665 and Andersonville Prison Records # 44609

[172] Massachusetts Soldiers, Sailors, and Marines in the Civil War, Vol. IV, pg. 681 and Andersonville Prison Records # 44619

54th Massachusetts (Continued)

- ○ **James Caldwell**, Private, Company H – Battle Creek, Michigan – 19 (also listed as 22) – Blacksmith – Enlisted 4-17-1863 – Captured at James Island, South Carolina on 7-16-1863 – Exchanged at Goldsboro, North Carolina on 3-4-1865 – Mustered out 6-7-1865 at Boston, Massachusetts[173]

- ○ **Jason Champlin**, Private, Company K – Shutesbury, Massachusetts – 30 – Farmer – Enlisted 7-13-1863 – Captured at Olustee, Florida on 2-20-1864[174]

- ○ **George Counsel** (also listed as Consel), Company B – Philadelphia, Pennsylvania – 27 (also listed as 37) – Laborer – Enlisted 2-25-1863 (also listed as 3-30-1863) – Captured at James Island, South Carolina on 7-16-1863 – Exchanged 3-4-1865 at Goldsboro, South Carolina – Returned to Company on 6-7-1865 –Mustered out 9-20-1865[175]

- ○ **John W. Dickinson**, Private, Company H – Galesburg, Illinois – 30 – Laborer Enlisted 4-26-1863 (also listed as 5-13-1863) – Captured at James Island, South Carolina on 7-16-1863 – Exchanged 3-4-1865 at Goldsboro, North Carolina – Mustered out 9-20-1865[176]

---

[173] Massachusetts Soldiers, Sailors, and Marines in the Civil War, Vol. IV, pg. 695 and Andersonville Prison Records # 63935

[174] Massachusetts Soldiers, Sailors, and Marines in the Civil War, Vol. IV, pg. 706 and Andersonville Prison Records # 43038

[175] Massachusetts Soldiers, Sailors, and Marines in the Civil War, Vol. IV, pg. 665 and Andersonville Prison Records # 44610

[176] Massachusetts Soldiers, Sailors, and Marines in the Civil War, Vol. IV, pg. 696 and Andersonville Prison Records # 44625

54th Massachusetts (Continued)

- ○ **Jefferson Ellis**, Private, Company F – Poughkeepsie, New York – 19 – Boatman – Enlisted 4-4-1863 (also listed as 4-23-1863) – Captured at Fort Wagner on 7-18-1863 – Exchanged at Goldsboro, North Carolina on 3-4-1865 – Mustered out 9-20-1865[177]

- ○ **Ralph B. Gardner**, Company A-- Great Barrington, Mass. – 23 – Laborer – Enlisted 2-18-1863 (also listed as 3-30-1863) – Captured at Fort Wagner, South Carolina on 7-18-1863 – Exchanged on 3-4-1865 – Discharged on 7-27-1865 from U.S. General Hospital, Annapolis, Maryland[178]

- ○ **George Grant**, Private, Company B – Philadelphia, Pennsylvania – 20 – Farmer Enlisted 3-3-1863 (also listed as 3-30-1863) – Captured at Fort Wagner, South Carolina on 7-18-1863 – Exchanged on 3-4-1865 at Goldsboro, North Carolina – Discharged on 6-24-1865 at Camp Parole, Annapolis, Maryland[179]

- ○ **Alfred Green**, Private, Company B – Hollidaysburg, Pennsylvania – 26 – Farmer Enlisted 3-11-1863 (also listed s 3-30-1863) Captured at Fort Wagner, South Carolina on 7-18-1863 – Exchanged on 3-4-1865 at Goldsboro, North Carolina[180]

---

[177] Massachusetts Soldiers, Sailors, and Marines in the Civil War, Vol. IV, pg. 685 and Andersonville Prison Records # 64844
[178] Massachusetts Soldiers, Sailors, and Marines in the Civil War, Vol. IV, pg. 660 and Andersonville Prison Records # 65201
[179] Massachusetts Soldiers, Sailors, and Marines in the Civil War, Vol. IV, pg. 666 and Andersonville Prison Records # 65363
[180] Massachusetts Soldiers, Sailors, and Marines in the Civil War, Vol. IV, pg. 666 and Andersonville Prison Records # 44611

54th Massachusetts (Continued)

- o **William Grover**, Private, Company E – Hartford, Connecticut – 18 – Farmer – Enlisted 4-4-1863 (also listed as 4-22-1863) – Captured at Fort Wagner, South Carolina on 7-18-1863 – Died in prison at Florence, South Carolina on or about 2-21-1865[181]

- o **Charles Hardy**, Private, Company B – Philadelphia, Pennsylvania – 20 – Laborer – Enlisted 2-18-1863 (also listed as 3-30-1863) Captured at Fort Wagner, South Carolina on 7-18-1863 – Died on 3-18-1865 in unknown Confederate prison[182]

- o **Hill Harris**, Private, Company G – Jackson, Florida – 26 – Farmer – Enlisted 4-14-1863 (also listed as 4-23-1863) – Captured at Honey Hill, South Carolina on 11-30-1864 – Released 4-25-1865 – Mustered out 9-20- 1865 from Boston, Massachusetts[183]

- o **William Henry Harrison**, Company H – Galesburg, Illinois – 35 – Teamster – Enlisted 4-26-1863 – Captured at James Island, South Carolina on 7-16-1863 – Died in prison in Florence, South Carolina on 1-26-1865[184]

---

[181] Massachusetts Soldiers, Sailors, and Marines in the Civil War, Vol. IV, pg. 682 and Andersonville Prison Records # 44620

[182] Massachusetts Soldiers, Sailors, and Marines in the Civil War, Vol. IV, pg. 666 and Andersonville Prison Records # 44612

[183] Massachusetts Soldiers, Sailors, and Marines in the Civil War, Vol. IV, pg. 691

[184] Massachusetts Soldiers, Sailors, and Marines in the Civil War, Vol. IV, pg. 696 and Andersonville Prison Records # 44626

54th Massachusetts (Continued)

- **Isaac S. Hawkins**, Private, Company D – Medina, New York – 29 – Sailor – Enlisted 12-12-1863 – Captured at Olustee, Florida on 2-20-1864 – Exchanged 3-24-1865 at Northeast Ferry, North Carolina – Discharged 6-20-1865 at Camp Parole, Annapolis, Maryland[185]

- **Cornelius Henson**, Private, Company C – New Bedford, Massachusetts – 22 – Laborer – Enlisted 2-28-1863 (also listed as 3-30-1863) – Captured at Fort Wagner, South Carolina on 7-18-1863 – Exchanged on 3-4-1865 at Wilmington, North Carolina – Discharged on 7-8-1865 at Boston, Massachusetts[186]

- **William F. Hill**, Private, Company A – Sherborn, Massachusetts – 18 – Student – Enlisted 3-10-1863 (also listed as 3-30-1863) – Captured at Fort Wagner, South Carolina on 7-18-1863 – Died in prison at Florence, South Carolina[187]

- **Nathaniel Hurley**, Private, Company E – Rochester, New York – 19 – Laborer Enlisted 3-29-1863 (also listed as 4-23-1863) – Captured at Fort Wagner, South Carolina on 7-18-1863 – Died in prison in Florence, South Carolina on or about 2-5-1865[188]

---

[185]Massachusetts Soldiers, Sailors, and Marines in the Civil War, Vol. IV, pg. 677 and Andersonville Prison Records # 41355
[186] Massachusetts Soldiers, Sailors, and Marines in the Civil War, Vol. IV, pg. 672 and Andersonville Prison Records # 55618 & 44618
[187] Massachusetts Soldiers, Sailors, and Marines in the Civil War, Vol. IV, pg. 661 and Andersonville Prison Record # 65828
[188] Massachusetts Soldiers, Sailors, and Marines in the Civil War, Vol. IV, pg. 682 and Andersonville Prison Records # 44621

- o **Walter Jefferies**, Private, Company H – Cincinnati, Ohio – 38 – Laborer – Enlisted 4-29-1863 – Captured at James Island, South Carolina on 7-16-1863 – Exchanged 3-4-1865 at Goldsboro, South Carolina – Mustered out 9-20-1865[189]

- o **Edward Johnson**, Private, Company G – Evansville, Indiana – 33 – Laborer – Enlisted 7-25-1863 – Captured at Olustee, Florida on 2-20-1864 – Exchanged 4-15-1865 – Discharged on disability on 7-16-1865 at Beaufort, South Carolina[190]

- o **Moses Johnson** (also listed as M. Johnston), Private, Company B – Philadelphia, Pennsylvania – 28 – Laborer – Enlisted 3-4-1863 – Captured at Olustee, Florida on 2-20-1864 – Originally recorded as having died at Andersonville and buried in Grave # 5437, changed by quartermaster to "reported to have died" in 1913[191]

- o **Henry Kirk**, Private, Company H – Galesburg, Illinois – 22 – Laborer – Enlisted 4-26-1863 – Captured at James Island, South Carolina on 7-16-1863 – Exchanged on 3-4-1865 at Goldsboro, North Carolina – Mustered out 7-27-1865 at Parole, Annapolis, Maryland[192]

---

[189] Massachusetts Soldiers, Sailors, and Marines in the Civil War, Vol. IV, pg. 697 and Andersonville Prison Records # 44627

[190] Massachusetts Soldiers, Sailors, and Marines in the Civil War, Vol. IV, pg. 692 and Andersonville Prison Records # 44623

[191] Massachusetts Soldiers, Sailors, and Marines in the Civil War, Vol. IV, pg. 667 and Andersonville Prison Record # 67241

[192] Massachusetts Soldiers, Sailors, and Marines in the Civil War, Vol. IV, pg. 697 and Andersonville Prison Record # 44628

54th Massachusetts (Continued)

- **John Leatherman**, Private, Company H – Ypsilanti, Michigan – 24 – Seaman – Enlisted 4-21-1863 – Captured at James Island, South Carolina on 7-16-1863 – Exchanged on 3-4-1865 at Goldsboro, North Carolina – Mustered out on 9-20-1865[193]

- **William Mitchell**, Private, Company F – Oberlin, Ohio – 27 – Farmer – Enlisted 4-18-1863 (also listed as April 23, 1863) – Captured at Olustee, Florida on 2-20-1864 – In Confederate Hospital in Lake City, Florida – Died, in Florida, date unknown – Dropped from rolls on 7-26-1864[194]

- **George Morris**, Private, Company B – Philadelphia, Pennsylvania – 22 – Sailor -- Enlisted 3-3-1863 – Captured at Olustee, Florida on 2-20-1864 – Sent to Columbia, South Carolina on 2-28-1865 – Exchanged 3-4-1865 at Goldsboro, North Carolina – Rejoined his company on 6-5-1865 from Parole, Annapolis, Maryland[195]

- **William H. Morris**, Private, Company K – New Bedford, Massachusetts – 22 –Sailor – Enlisted 9-1-1863 – Captured at Olustee, Florida on 2-20-1864[196]

---

[193] Massachusetts Soldiers, Sailors, and Marines in the Civil War, Vol. IV, pg. 697 and Andersonville Prison Record # 44629

[194] Massachusetts Soldiers, Sailors, and Marines in the Civil War, Vol. IV, pg. 687 and Andersonville Prison Record # 43253

[195] Massachusetts Soldiers, Sailors, and Marines in the Civil War, Vol. IV, pg. 667 and Andersonville prison Record # 44613

[196] Massachusetts Soldiers, Sailors, and Marines in the Civil War, Vol. IV, pg. 708 and Andersonville Prison Record # 43262

- **George W. Moshroe**, Company F – Elmira, New York – 23 – Laborer Enlisted 4-8-1863 (also listed as 4-23-1863) – Captured at Fort Wagner, South Carolina on 7-18-1863 – Exchanged at Goldsboro, North Carolina on 3-4-1865 – Mustered out 9-20-1865[197]

- **Joseph Proctor**, Private, Company H – Chambersburg, Pennsylvania – 24 – Cook – Enlisted 4-21-1863 – Captured at James Island, South Carolina on 7-18-1863 – Exchanged 3-4-1865 at Goldsboro, North Carolina – Discharged 6-23-1865 at Parole, Annapolis, Maryland – Buried in Lincoln Cemetery in Chambersburg, Pennsylvania[198]

- **George T. Prosser**, Private, Company D – Columbia, Pennsylvania – 21 – Laborer – Enlisted 3-19-1863 (also listed as 3-30-1863) – Captured at Olustee, Florida on 2-20-1864 – Exchanged at Goldsboro, North Carolina on 3-4-1865 – Rejoined company on 6-7-1865 – Mustered out 9-20- 1865[199]

- **A. Ratsall**, Private, Company H – Muster and capture information unknown – Escaped on 9-27-1864[200]

---

[197] Massachusetts Soldiers, Sailors, and Marines in the Civil War, Vol. IV, pg. 686 and Andersonville Prison Record # 44622
[198] Massachusetts Soldiers, Sailors, and Marines in the Civil War, Vol. IV, pg. 698 and Andersonville Prison Records # 44630
[199] Massachusetts Soldiers, Sailors, and Marines in the Civil War, Vol. IV, pg. 678 and Andersonville Prison Record # 67760
[200] Andersonville Prison Records # 58376

54th Massachusetts (Continued)

- o **William Rigby**, Private, Company B --West Chester, Pennsylvania – 21 – Farmer – Enlisted 3-11-1863 (also listed as 3-30-1863) – Captured at Fort Wagner, South Carolina on 7-18-1863 – Exchanged 3-4-1865 at Goldsboro, North Carolina – Discharged on 6-24-1865 at Parole, Annapolis, Maryland [201]

- o **Robert Riley** (also listed as James Riley) Private, Company H – Chicago, Illinois – 17 – Farmer – Enlisted 4-21-1863[202]

- o **Enos Smith**, Private, Company H – Easton, Pennsylvania – 30 – Laborer – Enlisted 4-21-1863 – Captured at James Island, South Carolina on 7-16-1863 – Died in prison in Florence, South Carolina[203]

- o **Charles Stanton**, Private, Company G – Glen Falls, New York – 21 – Boatman – Enlisted on 4-9-1863 – Captured at Fort Wagner, South Carolina on 7-18-1863 – Died in prison in Florence, South Carolina on 2-25-1865[204]

- o **Daniel States**, Company B – Philadelphia, Pennsylvania – 18 – Farmer – Enlisted 2-27-1863 (also listed as 3-30-1863) – Captured at Fort Wagner, South Carolina on 7-18-1863 – Exchanged on 3-4-1865 at Goldsboro, North Carolina – Mustered out 9-20-1865 [205]

---

[201] Massachusetts Soldiers, Sailors, and Marines in the Civil War, Vol. IV, pg. 668 and Andersonville prison Record # 44614

[202] Massachusetts Soldiers, Sailors, and Marines in the Civil War, Vol. IV, pg. 698 and Andersonville Prison Records # 58688

[203] Massachusetts Soldiers, Sailors, and Marines in the Civil War, Vol. IV, pg. 698 and Andersonville Prison Records # 44631

[204] Massachusetts Soldiers, Sailors, and Marines in the Civil War, Vol. IV, pg. 694 and Andersonville Prison Records # 44624

[205] Massachusetts Soldiers, Sailors, and Marines in the Civil War, Vol. IV, pg. 668 and Andersonville Prison Record # 44615

54th Massachusetts (Continued)

- **George W. Thomas** (also George H.), Private, Company F – Buffalo, New York – 19 – Sailor – Enlisted 4-8-1863 (also listed 4-23-1863) – Captured at Fort Wagner on 7-18-1863 Exchanged on 3-4-1865 at Goldsboro, North Carolina – Mustered out on 9-20-1865[206]

- **Frederick Wallace**, Private, Company H – Cincinnati, Ohio – 20 – Barber – Enlisted 4-21-1863 (also listed as 5-13-1863) – Captured at James Island, South Carolina on 7-16-1863 – Exchanged on 3-4-1865 at Goldsboro, North Carolina – Discharged 6-7-1865 at St. Andrews Parish, South Carolina[207]

- **Alfred Whiting**, Sgt., Company I – Carlisle, Pennsylvania – 23 – Waiter – Enlisted 4-22-1863 (also listed as 5-13-1863) – Captured at Fort Wagner, South Carolina on 7-18-1863 – Exchanged on 3-4-1865 at Goldsboro, North Carolina – Died on 6-26-1865 at unknown location and from unknown causes [208]

- **Charles S. Williams**, Private, Company B – Philadelphia, Pennsylvania – 20 – Bricklayer – Enlisted 3-14-1863 (also listed as 3-30-1863) Captured at Fort Wagner, South Carolina on 7-18-1863 – Died in prison in Florence, South Carolina on or about 1-15-1865[209]

---

[206] Massachusetts Soldiers, Sailors, and Marines in the Civil War, Vol. IV, pg. 689 and Andersonville Prison Records # 68825

[207] Massachusetts Soldiers, Sailors, and Marines in the Civil War, Vol. IV, pg. 699 and Andersonville Prison Record # 44632

[208] Massachusetts Soldiers, Sailors, and Marines in the Civil War, Vol. IV, pg. 705 and Andersonville Prison Records # 44634

[209] Massachusetts Soldiers, Sailors, and Marines in the Civil War, Vol. IV, pg. 669 and Andersonville Prison Records # 44617

- **James O. Williams**, Private, Company H – Carlisle, PA – 35 – Farmer – Enlisted 4-15-1863 (also listed as 3-30-1863) – Captured at Fort Wagner, South Carolina on 7-18-1863 – Died in prison in Florence, South Carolina[210]

- **Samuel R. Wilson**, Private, Company B – West Chester, Pennsylvania – 21 – Farmer – Enlisted 3-9-1863 – Captured at Fort Wagner, South Carolina on 7-18-1863 – Died in prison at Florence, South Carolina[211]

- **Stewart W. Woods**, Private, Company I – Carlisle, Pennsylvania – 27 – Laborer – Enlisted 4-29-1863 (also listed as 5-13-1863) – Captured at Fort Wagner on 7-18-1863 – Exchanged on 3-4-1865 at Goldsboro, North Carolina – Died on 3-15-1865 in Wilmington, North Carolina[212]

- **Henry W. Worthington**, Private, Company H – Defiance, Ohio – 18 – Laborer – Enlisted 5-12-1863 – Captured at James Island, South Carolina on 7-16-1863 – Died in prison in Florence, South Carolina on 1-8-1865[213]

---

[210] Massachusetts Soldiers, Sailors, and Marines in the Civil War, Vol. IV, pg. 699 and Andersonville Prison Records # 44633

[211] Massachusetts Soldiers, Sailors, and Marines in the Civil War, Vol. IV, pg. 670 and Andersonville Prison Records # 44617

[212] Massachusetts Soldiers, Sailors, and Marines in the Civil War, Vol. IV, pg. 705 and Andersonville Prison Records # 44635

[213] Massachusetts Soldiers, Sailors, and Marines in the Civil War, Vol. IV, pg. 700 and Andersonville Prison Records # 69476

137th USCT

- o **John Proctor**, Private, Company B[214]
- o **Stephen Saltmarsh**, Private, Company G[215]
- o **Daniel Sanders** – Died 4-8-1864[216]
- o **William Scott**, Private, Company D[217]

---

[214] Andersonville Prison Records # 43472
[215] Andersonville Prison Records # 43329
[216] Andersonville Prison Records # 30447 – many prisoner's records do not match actual burial records. Sanders may have died at Andersonville, but the prison records do not indicate that he died there.
[217] Andersonville Prison Records # 43340

Other notes on Andersonville Prison

It is interesting to note that three of the 8th USCT were called to testify in the trial of the Andersonville prison commandant Henry Wirz[218] in August – November, 1865 in Washington.[219] Those three were William Jennings, a private in Company A, George Washington, a private in Company E and John Fisher, a private in Company B. About 160 witnesses testified.[220] It is not certain whether any of the three actually testified or not. One newspaper account of the Wirz Trial tells of testimony of a colored Andersonville prisoner Frank Mattox, 35th USCT (1st North Carolina) who "testified to the cruelties inflicted upon himself and others of his color."[221]

Blacks were not allowed to testify in a court of law according to the Dred Scott Decision (March of 1857)[222] but the Wirz trial was a military trial. (Blacks also testified in the military trial of the Lincoln conspirators earlier that same year in Washington.)[223]

Twelve of the 54th Massachusetts USCT were transferred from Andersonville Prison to the prison in Florence, South Carolina. Included in that group were David Bailey, Morris Butler, William Grover, William Henry

---

[218] Henry Wirz was the commandant of Andersonville Prison who was tried, found guilty and executed in 1865. Andersonville Georgia USA, pg. 15

[219] The trial started on August 21, 1865. Henry Wirz was sentenced on November 6 and was hanged on November 10 at the Old Capitol Prison. *Harpers Weekly*, September 16, 1865 and *Harpers Weekly*, November 25, 1865.

[220] Andersonville Prison and the Captain Henry Wirz Trial, pg. 15.

[221] *Harpers Weekly*, September 16, 1865

[222] Dred Scott Decision –John Brown's Trial, pg. 236

[223] The Lincoln Conspirators trials were held from May 1 – June 30, 1865. Eighteen of the witnesses (ten for the prosecution and eight for the defense) of Dr. Samuel Alexander Mudd were listed as "coloreds" including several former slaves of the Mudd family. The Trial, pgs. LXXXI, v. & xii.

Harrison, William F. Hill, Nathaniel Hurley, Enos Smith, Charles Stanton, Charles Williams, James O. Williams, Samuel R. Wilson, and Henry W. Worthington. While they had all survived their stay at Andersonville, the twelve USCT transferred from Andersonville to Florence all died in the Florence Stockade, also called the Confederates States Military Prison at Florence, within one month of their transfer.

The prison at Florence held over 18,000 Union prisoners, with 2,802 reported to have died in the stockade. They are buried in unmarked trenches within the Florence National Cemetery. The Florence Stockade received many of the Union prisoners from Andersonville Prison after it was determined around Sept. 1, 1864 to move the prisoners due to Andersonville being a possible target for General Sherman's army.[224]

At Andersonville, the USCT soldiers were given rations to keep them healthy. They received exercise each day and were allowed to leave the prison to work in the cemetery to dig graves.

When the prison was closed in early 1865, there were no USCT soldiers at the prison. They had been transferred out.

[224] Andersonville Diary, p. 175.

Cemetery at Andersonville

Remarkably, almost all the graves at Andersonville are marked with headstones.

The records were compiled by prisoner Dorence Atwater who not only compiled the data on each prisoner who died in the encampment, but copied the list so that when he left the list would survive too.

When Clara Barton heard of Atwater's list, she petitioned the Commissary General of Prisoners Hoffman to send a delegation to Andersonville to mark the graves. She insisted that both she and Mr. Atwater be sent along. Captain James Moore was ordered to lead the delegation. That group included two clerks, one foreman, twelve carpenters, twelve letterers, and seven laborers. They proceeded to put a wooden marker on each grave to preserve its identity. The enclave arrived at the prison on July 25, 1865 and worked until 12,920 graves were marked for posterity.[225] (The official total is 12,912 including four hundred forty-three unknown Union soldiers.) [226]

Later, the wooden markers were all replaced with the markers there today.

---

[225] Andersonville, Georgia USA, pgs. 47-51.
[226] Andersonville Diary, pg. 287

Special Thanks

This project could not have been accomplished without the urging and assistance of Renee and Kevin Frye of Andersonville Prison. Renee, who manages the book store for Eastern National, actually encouraged me to write this book. And Kevin, a National Park Service volunteer extraordinaire at Andersonville, helped substantiate the data I already had and added significantly to it. Those are Kevin's excellent photographs throughout the booklet.

Thank you – Renee and Kevin. You are the best!!!!

I continue to be grateful for all the support and love that my family and friends provide for me on a daily basis. I also continue to be grateful to my teacher, Rebecca Boreczky who lit the fire I needed to become a published author.

Special Note

This booklet is a work in progress. I would appreciate any additional information, corrections or additions on any of the soldiers included or any who might have been inadvertently left out.

My ultimate goal here is to provide the best available information in the most correct form. I will be updating the information periodically as new information becomes available.

If you have any information relating to the USCT at Andersonville, please contact me by e-mail.

author@boboconnorbooks.com

About the Author

I live in Charles Town, West Virginia and have worked in the tourism industry since the early 1980s, with assignments in the center of the Civil War battles. I parlayed both interests into the publishing of historical fiction accounts of the Civil War.

My interest in Andersonville Prison dates back to a visit several years ago when my friend Antonia Camp took me to the prison. Since then I have visited several times and have actually slept in the stockade in a shebang. My fascination of the U.S. Colored Troops comes from my studies of Abraham Lincoln, slavery, and Martin Delany. My book "Catesby: Eyewitness to the Civil War" offers a historical fiction look at the USCT at Andersonville Prison.

Please check out my other books published by Infinity Publishing:

"The Perfect Steel Trap – Harpers Ferry 1859"
Finalist 2006 Best Book Awards

"The Virginian Who Might Have Saved Lincoln"
Also available on Audio Book – Finalist Indie Excellence Awards and Finalist 2007 Best Book Awards

"Catesby – Eyewitness to the Civil War"

Please visit my website at
www.boboconnorbooks.com

Bibliography

Bates, Samuel P – The History of the Pennsylvania Volunteers, 1861-1865, Volume V.

Brown, William Wells – The Negro in the American Rebellion, 1867

Chapman, N. P. – The Tragedy of Andersonville, The Henry Wirz Trial, The Prison Keeper, 1911

Dann, Martin E., Editor – The Black Press, 1827-1890, G. P. Putman's Sons, New York, 1971

Gladstone, William A. – United States Colored Troops, Thomas Publications, Gettysburg, Pa. 1990

Gross, Warren Lee – The Soldier's Story of His Captivity at Andersonville, Belle Island and other Rebel Prisons, 1870

Lardas, Mark – African American Soldier in the Civil War, USCT 1862-66, Osprey Publishing Ltd. New York, New York, 2006

McGinty, Brian – John Brown's Trial, Harvard University Press, Cambridge, Mass., 2009

McPherson, James M. – The Negro's Civil War, Pantheon Books, New York, 1965

Pagadis, James M. – Strike a Blow for Freedom, The 6th U.S. Colored Infantry in the Civil War, White Mane Books, Shippensburg, PA., 2000

Ransom. John L. – Andersonville Diary, with list of the dead, Published by the author, Auburn, N.Y., originally published in 1881, reprinted by DSI Digital Reproduction, 2003

Sheppard, Peggy – Andersonville, Georgia USA, Sheppard Publications, Andersonville, Georgia, 1973

Smith, John David, editor – Black Soldiers in Blue, African American Troops in the Civil War Era, University of North Carolina Press, 2002

Emancipation Proclamation

Harpers Weekly, September 16, 1865

Harpers Weekly, November 25, 1865

Massachusetts Adjutant General's Office, Massachusetts Soldiers, Sailors and Marines in the Civil War, Vol. IV

Official Records, Andersonville Prison

Publication Number M-1821 – Compiled Military Service Records of Volunteer Union Soldiers Who Served with the United States Colored Troops Infantry Organizations, 8th through 13th, including the 11th (new), 2000

Phister's Records of the Great Rebellion

The Trial – Edited by Edward Steers, Jr. – University Press of Kentucky, 2003

Andersonville Prison and the Captain Henry Wirz Trial, Reprinted from U.D.C. Bulletin originally published in 1921 entitled Facts and Figures vs. Myths and Misrepresentations Henry Wirz and Andersonville Prison

The Florence Stockade website

www.battleofolustee.org/letters/grace.html

www.battleofolustee.org/letters/bogle.htm

www.battleofolustee.org/letters/1stnc-1.htm

www.mycivilwar.com/pow/ga-millen.htm

www.learner.org/workshops/primarysources/emancipation/docs/jhgooding.html

www.angelfire.com/ga4/usct/35thusct.html

www.angelfire.com/ga4/usct/8thusct.html

www.angelfire.com/ga4/usct/17thusct.html

www.angelfire.com/ga4/usct/16thusct.html

www.pbs.org/wgbh/aia/part2/2p24.html

INDEX of USCT at Andersonville Prison

INDEX of USCT at Andersonville Prison (Continued)

INDEX of USCT at Andersonville Prison (Continued)

INDEX of USCT at Andersonville Prison (Continued)